Life After a Death

Navigating New Widowhood with Humor & Hope

Trina Machacek

For Jerry.
I Remember and I'm Alive
and
For My Friend Sue.
When I think of you and your faith,
You keep my feet on the ground.

Table of Contents

Introduction

Oh, what is with that name—Machacek? Don't worry if you can't pronounce it. When Jerry and I were married in 1976, even the preacher couldn't say it. He turned us around to the congregation and said, "May I now introduce to you the new Mr. & Mrs. Mackachawkeck." What a way to start a life together. Mrs. Mackachawkeck. Yeah, sound that one out! Anyway, here's how I tell people to pronounce it...

Machacek is Czechoslovakian. Jerry's family was Czech. And yes, he taught me a few of *those* words in Czech! The first "c" in Machacek is silent. Perhaps an example would help. Pretend you have no money and you write a hot check. After passing it across the counter, you're asked, "Is that your hot check?" In your best Southern twang, you reply, "Yep, that's ma hot check." Good, now say "ma hot check" faster. That's how you pronounce Machacek.

Married to Jerry, who was Czech—who I thought was hot— you could say he was *my* hot Czech. That's what I hear when I say aloud my last name. Over all the years, good times and bad, through it all, we loved each other. He was truly *my hot Czech*.

As you venture forth into my after-death life, you will occasionally come across little notes in **bold** or in neat, shadowed boxes. When you reach those, I want you to remember that at every turn, every stumble, and yes, every amazing celebration of your life, I am cheering you on.

It won't make everything in life perfect but sometimes knowing you aren't alone makes all the difference. The light at the end of the tunnel isn't a train. It's the sun waiting for you to join it. Let it shine and warm your soul.

1

1

Begin at the End

The beginning is such an awful and varied place to start a story, book, or a trip down memory lane. It's like picking a strawberry from a tangle of knotted vines contained within an overgrown patch of mixed grass and foliage. So many vines, flowers, leaves, and garbage plants to root through! You finally wrestle out a large, red eye-catching berry. You think this is the best strawberry and then you look down and there is another one, and another. Pretty soon you find there are too many strawberries to choose from. It's overwhelming to pick which is the best. So, sometimes you don't pick any at all.

That is what it has been like for me to pick a starting point. Who I am today is not who I was a few years ago. Before that one last breath was exhaled and shoved me into my new future. Of me becoming a widow, a single woman, a non-married person, a new *me*. The beginning can begin anywhere. The death of my husband was the beginning of my life, after a death.

I had just finished reading a couple of stories Carolyn, a friend from southern California, sent me. One was from Truman Capote who, of course, wrote wonderful but strange books like *In Cold Blood* and *Breakfast at Tiffany's*. The story she sent me though was one about a memory he had of an odd relative and the last Christmas he spent with her. The story hit home because the first story I wrote that delivered me on my writing path was also about a Christmas memory. How did that happen?

The second story waiting for me in that same packet detailed how author Harper Lee had received a grand Christmas gift from a couple with which she had been living. The gift was enough money to take a year off from work to write the book that brought her into the spotlight, *To Kill a Mockingbird*. During that time, she also wrote a book that had been bubbling in her head waiting to burst forth. She had needed some sort of push to get it on paper.

Sort of like the story I am telling here. That bubbling is insuppressible as it longs to make its way into our reality. Again, how was it that these two stories found their way to my living room at a time I needed that same push in my life?

After devouring the shared materials, I looked up both authors to learn more about them. I discovered they had known each other as children and had been good friends. Both told of journeys they had undergone together, sometimes with contradicting details. Despite these discrepancies, their stories were touching, poignant. And one thing became abundantly clear to me—it was time to pick a starting point and create the book that I had been desperately shoving away because I was too scared to let it surface. Afraid it wasn't worth it, not what anyone really wants to hear or read. That I was not the person to tell it, let alone good enough to write it in a way that helped newbies of widowhood realize they were going to make it through this horrible maze. And come out stronger on the other end.

That person, that person who is scared and demure?

That person is definitely not who I am.

So, in my friend's not-so-subtle way, she was screaming at me to get my head out of my butt and, quite frankly, stop trying to be everything to everyone. Just sit down and put on paper all the thoughts, trials, errors, laughable events, crying jags—oh, just all the things that have been bubbling in my gray matter for some time. That is, to put into words what it is like to become a new person draped in what are sometimes dark, drab clothing but also bright shining newness that now makes me a widow. AARRGGHH I hate that word. *Widow.* Unfortunately, I have to say that crummy word many more times; it cuts sharply each time.

I want to say this about becoming the new me. I did not just—*poof*—become new. After a while, I just kind of hatched. Yep, like one of those mint-green shelled eggs from an Araucana Easter Egg Chicken. An egg that had been incubating for more years than it takes to grow one of those huge trees which is sacrificed annually to proclaim the nation will celebrate Christmas. Then again, eggs are a new beginning, a start of something that, if handled with care, can actually go on forever. Egg, chicken, egg, chicken, egg, uh, rooster. Well, there has to be a rooster and a hen! That's just basic health class.

Really, life *does* start as an egg. And it *does* take a long time to become who we are, to become something beautiful from just an egg. Consider this:

When my husband Jerry died in January 2018, an indescribable sadness covered my world, but I did not let it define me. I still have a hard time saying out loud, "He died." Those words get stuck in my throat; I don't know if that will ever change. I hope so but not yet. He died; I didn't. Well, of course, *part* of me died. Come on, I am not heartless. I just learned that life is part of death and death is part of life. Getting from there to here was a journey I would not heap upon friend or foe. It happened though and now, after a few years of icky widowhood under my belt, I am finally at a peaceful place (okay, okay—at a peaceful place *for the most part*), in a calm-ish position, and have a burning desire, a deep-seated need, to talk about some stuff.

It's going to be a corker, a crying fest, a laugh along the way, a somewhat quiet, a sometimes very loud, always truthful and sometimes eye-popping ride.

Hang on to your bloomers. Here we go. Together.
Don't worry, I got ya.

2

Who Am I Now?

I now have to identify with so many aspects of life. Most of which I am not that thrilled about. As I said, and will always say, I do not like the word widow. I do not like being single. I do not like being the third or fifth or seventh person at a table. But! Yes, I will add a "but" wherever I dang-well please. But all the days of my life from here on out are mine to do with as I desire. I have to get used to telling myself it is okay to say it is all about me. Not only that but to be okay in saying and feeling this:

What I do from here on out will define me.

My, how time flies when you are living. My life, like what yours might be, was regular, exciting, mundane, and amazing. All those adjectives and more, so much more. Along the path of life, people marry, cohabitate, shack up, whatever you call it; and something made you one part of a twosome. Oh, but then it happened.

It.

Death.

It is powerful. *It* is big. *It* is something unimaginable. *It* happens all the time... Too someone else. A neighbor. A sister. A friend of your mom's. Maybe even your mom. Or dad. *It* happens to the lady or man down the street, across the way, around the corner. Father Time shows Death where you live and he swoops down, knocks heavily with a wicked hand, and you don't even have to lift a finger to answer the door.

No, Death lets itself in.

You think if you don't answer, it will just evaporate and go away? Ha, I tried that. Let me know how that goes for you. No matter if you answer that knock or not, Death will barge in with a whoosh of air that is as foul as the air when you drive down the road next to some unseen sewer ponds.

In life you are traveling along just fine and dandy. Then your nose is accosted by something that sadly is not unfamiliar. Try as you might, you can't get away from it fast enough. That is what is behind the door of Death. Even when you get past the first stench and stink of *It*, you fear you can really never shake it. No matter how fast you drive or how hard you dance in life. I was juggling ten balls in the air with illness, work, medicines, family, house, bills. I thought if I just kept juggling and kept all the balls in the air, things would keep going.

Juggle, dance, juggle, dance. Then? It is like passing that sewer pond; you know it immediately—yes, your nose knows that smell no matter how long it has been since it first entered your life. Death touches you.

Take heart. Trust that there is still fresh air to be had. This I can promise without any reservations. There is fresh air still to be had by you and your nose. Do not give into the pit you feel you're being sucked into. That stupid line you have heard or seen or read, "Just Keep Breathing," is pointed at your nose now. **Just keep breathing.** That breath of fresh air is the beginning of your new life when you become a widow.

Within these next pages, these next stories, these next reflections, I share some craggily trails meant to inform, entertain, and, to some extent, ease you or someone you know into the widowhood club. Or widower-hood. Is that a thing?

Oh, a widow. (I hate that word.) I am now, and forever will be, a widow. Dang it anyway.

3

WHY ME?

This isn't going to be about why you got to be the one in the barrel and became the newest widow on the block. That's a question with no real answer. So, quit trying to put any parameters around why you are in the position you are in. It will just drive you to be stuck in the muck. You need to realize **it is your turn**. Sounds hard, I know. Oh, *how* I *know*. But it is doable. It is. Promise.

I submit the question of "Why me—to write this book?" to be more along these lines. Because there are people who ask it. And I never shy away from explaining my silly self.

Why? Why am I here to spout about this journey? Why do I find a need, a desire, to reveal to the world the path from my husband's death to my new life? Why do I feel I can do this? Who am I to be able to talk, tell, share, inform, and hopefully ease you or someone you know or love along this path?

Because along my way, I have stumbled, I have risen, I have thought, *I wish there was someone out there I could ask all my weird, personal, outlandish, serious but mostly stupid questions to.* I would hunt that person down and invite her into my home and ask and ask and ask.

I am that person. I'm your gal.

There are tons, tons I say, of books about death and the aftermath and the journeys people take. I looked at some. Not many because I guess it just didn't suit me to read boo-hoo stories. Life was already a boo-hoo fest. Instead, I plodded along into my new life, occasionally feeling a bubbling in my brain. Something would happen and be dealt with in my own nearly always off-the-wall way. Then, that little voice in my head would say, "Oh, this is what I would have wanted to know about that. If there was just a guide, a book, a gathering of short non-preachy, to-the-point stories telling about the things that splat goo on the face of the one left behind." Now *that* is a book I would read.

I mentioned it a few times to friends, you know, like you do while talking and stuff. Over and over, I heard myself say, "Oh, I have this idea," "Oh, I think this about that," "Oh, maybe I can make that step in this process easier or at least not so insurmountable to someone who will certainly face this along the widow highway." Yes, those thoughts.

That is *this* book! I don't want to dwell on what was; I want to delve into what is and what is yet to come for those who, at the end of one life, are faced with and—yes, believe it or not—*blessed with* beginning a new adventure. Oh, trust me. It is an adventure in every sense of the word. Someone in your life dies and you begin that road to your very own "Life after a Death." Well, isn't that just peachy? Yikers!

Why I am that person to talk about the journey? I am not in any way smarter that you. I have not one square inch of sheepskin-inscribed diplomas on my wall touting anything more than life experiences. I am not a doctor, a therapist, a nurse, or a social worker. I was a CNA (Certified Nurse Assistant) for a short stint. I only took the course at a community college and got my nursing license so I would know how to do a few things I might come across in my life. Who knew I would have the distinct pleasure to use that knowledge to aid my husband on his last journey?

I dabble in writing. I have a weekly humor/lifestyle column called "Is This You?" in a few papers. It is a conglomeration of life events, stories, and remembrances that I get to share with readers. I like to think—now this will date me for sure— "Is This You?" is a cross between Baxter Black as a country theme and Erma Bombeck as a woman getting a big kick out of life. And of course, it is *all* about me. And some of my friends. I feel being a writer is a gift I have been blessed with. Within that realm, I can write about this newest journey I am on. And share it with you. I find that so cool and as rewarding as getting the corner brownie out of the pan. Yummy.

But no, I do not have any one thing any more special than any other woman who was a wife and then, through the acts of God and Death, became a non-wife. Someone who was a part of two and then—*poof*—became a one. I was one of two halves that made a whole, then I found I was standing there by myself.

This is a journey taken by millions of people every day, every stinking day. I just want to help make someone else's journey a titch less lonely. A little easier to swallow when things get so big in the middle of the night, when you are alone and it is dark and quiet. Let you know that alone really does suck. Alone is not all it is cracked up to be.

However, if you find yourself alone, take this to heart. The sun will come up after the night passes. The day dawns and that dang ole sun will shine on your face. Keep your eye on the prize. That yellow orb is sent to us each day to remind us that life can and does go on and it is warm and bright and given to you—like I said—every stinking day.

I also want to say that I do not have children. So, if you want to know anything about how to deal with the dynamics of children left behind, you are not going to get any help from me. I look at that as a blessing. Well, for the most part.

There *are* times when I wish I had children to lean on, to prop me up and have around to do some of the heavy lifting that life always has waiting around each corner. But I was not blessed with little Trinas or Jerrys, and so I cannot visualize my journey with those eyes. Nope, I am here to talk about being a woman or man. Not mom, daughter, sister, aunt, dad, son, or brother.

Just you and me.

After all, when the day is done, even if you have one or several children, it's still on your shoulders to bear the weight of this new life of yours. To put on that smile and step up and begin to live again.

Bahooie, you say?

You can't see yourself *ever* smiling again? You will *never* take a calm breath without it being ragged and too hard?

That is not true. That is not true. *That is not true!*

When Death happens, you are *never ready*! You have no idea what to ask at first. You have no idea all the tangles that stab at your heart, what is going to throw cold water on your face, or yes, even give you relief. Let's start there... The relief of it all.

4

Guilt of Relief

Yᴏᴜ should probably know this about me. I am very pragmatic. A quick check with a thesaurus will tell you that means I am all of these things: practical, realistic, rational, reasonable, down-to-earth, and hardheaded. Well, I'll happily take possession of that last one.

I love deeply and hold precious life in my hand and heart with the fierceness of Mother Earth cradling us all with the strength of gravity. I do not let go—until it is time.

If you have gone through your life up until this point and have never seen anyone die, count yourself both lucky and "in waiting." Pretty sure at some point, just like in that song or poem or whatever it was, a little rain will fall. Every person will experience the death of someone close to them. Chances are that a large percentage of the population will see the final act of a person played out in front of them.

Lucky me.

Yes, I was there when my other half took his last earthly breath and zoomed to Heaven. Yes, I believe in Heaven and God and Satan—and to some extent, Santa Clause and the Easter Bunny. My husband also believed in God. Okay, I might have, in my own way, helped him hold onto the fantasy of Santa and the Easter Bunny. But, he, in his own way, brought me closer to Christ. We were a grand twosome in that way. His stalwartness and my seat-of-the-pants, fly-away attitude kept us in check.

But Death comes nevertheless.

It can visit you in various forms—expected, unexpected, accident, intentional, terrible circumstances. No matter how it is delivered, you are **never ready**.

The circumstances of my journey with my husband in preparing him for the inevitable actually was, in some ways, borrowed from nearly every one of those. But in no way was it *intentional*. That one never played a part in his illness or death. Honestly, I cannot know how anyone deals with intentional death. I pray I never do.

My husband's name was Jerry. He was an amazing handful of a man with whom I shared 41 years, 8 months, and one day wed to. But who's counting?

He was a taskmaster, strong. In his prime, he could pick up 300 pounds of steel and weld it to another piece in the one-man machine shop he and I built. Yes, he was *that* strong. That shop was constructed along a 923-acre swath of dirt in Diamond Valley he had taken out of sagebrush. Ten miles north of Eureka, Nevada, the land was wonderfully beautiful in a high-desert, cold-in-the-winter and hot-in-the-summer kind of way.

After Jerry's father got prostate cancer and died in 1988, Jerry and I began reflecting on our lives together. It occurred to us that if something happened to him, I would be—without him doing the work he so loved in the machine shop—left without a way to make a living. Well, of course, I could get a job. I am a capable person and no slouch in the working arena. But he wanted to be more practical and take grown-up steps to take care of "the little woman." AKA me!

So, over the next few years, we worked toward building a plan for me. And in some ways for him too. After all, if I was called to Heaven first, he needed insurance as he was 11 years older than yours truly. Our path brought us to buying a few empty lots on Main Street, erecting a new building in Eureka, and opening a True Value Hardware store in 1993.

Eureka was a small community boasting about 1,400 residents within its 5,000-square-mile county at the time. We Eurekans sat smack dab in the center of Nevada. Despite being sparely population, Eureka County was—and has—a community with a heart of gold. Both metaphorically and legitimately. People will open up and give your heart anything when you are in need.

These days, Eureka is per capita in tax revenue also the richest county in the country as it has the biggest goldmines in the U.S. So the tax base is nice for the residents. New schools, new county facilities, and a fluctuating population of good, hard-working goldmine and county workers along with farmers and auxiliary working men and women make for a stable community. The mines spend good money as does Eureka County, Eureka School District, and the wonderful farmers who live here.

Well, come on now, Trina! It *is* a small community; there's bound to be someone not happy with a store or business or farm or whatever is going on in the county. Heck, I happily admit there is one store here I refuse to enter. Hopefully, I will never have to eat these words; I hope I never have to set foot inside the doors of that one store.

Wait a moment. I'd like to take a sidebar.

Remember, I'm going to be honest with you along this journey. I have feelings and I do not back down from them. The truth is so freeing, after all. For many, many years, I lived with secrets and closed minds. But now?

Now, I live by this—if I tell the truth, I don't have to have a good memory. Especially since I no longer have someone looking over my shoulder telling me what to say and what *not* to say. As a widow, it is all about **me** and **you** being the people we deem we want to be. Be the "you" that you want to become. Be your very own you. It's okay to step up and own your "you-ness." You are amazing—be your amazing you.

Sidebar over.

For the most part, we get along here in Eureka and really do look out for each other. That is what I love about living here.

Jerry and I saw a need in Eureka and we had a need to expand our livelihood, so Eureka True Value became what I still

13

love to think was a good addition to the community. Once we finished constructing the store, we finally opened in June 1993.

As the store grew, the time it took to run it increased. One thing we did not take into account when we started was the amount of time that is required to run a store. Just keeping up with the ordering and restocking was a daylight-to-after-dark job on Tuesdays and Wednesdays. I remember one evening working in the plumbing aisle. I was down on my hands and knees trying to read the tiny numbers off the tags for the four-inch PVC fittings to reorder them. When I went to get up, it was kind of hard. My legs didn't work quite right; there was a definite lack of strength that I had never noticed before. *No matter*, I told myself. *I just haven't eaten. It's nothing.*

After a True Value order was placed, a few days of rest each week followed until the delivery truck came in. Then all hands were on deck to unload and begin putting stuff away. It was a busy but rewarding time. We had some amazing people work with us. I still see, write to, and keep in touch with many of the employees we were lucky enough to have walk through our door and ask for a job.

We scooted along, singing our song of hardware for a few years and slowly the one-man machine shop, Machacek Iron Works (circa 1977), became secondary to the hardware store. He was 64 years old when the first signs of his illness came along.

In fall 1997, Jerry was unloading a truck. While guiding 350-pounds of dog food on a hand truck down a ramp, he felt a twinge in his back. He had never felt any type of pain before. Anywhere. Ever.

When he was diagnosed with Type II Diabetes in the 1980s, he kept on going as if nothing had changed. Once, he dropped a 350-pound piece of steel from a John Deere Swather reel on top of his foot. Broke eight bones and had each toe pinned but never missed a project deadline. The man was never sick or in pain. But that damned load of dog food caused a *twinge* in his back.

That twinge put him to bed that night and by the next morning—the very next morning—he could not get up. He crawled to the bathroom. It really was the beginning of a road that lasted the following 21 years.

The next week or so, that twinge was diagnosed as spinal stenosis. Something that, at that time, seemed nobody in our circle of family and friends had ever heard of. He was flown out by air ambulance from Eureka to a hospital in Elko, Nevada where they poked and prodded at him for a couple of days.

Now here, I need to insert a little about the start of my own journey of his illness. We were full on into running the hardware store, and blessed that our employees were wonderful and took over for us when we needed them. I did not fly in the air ambulance to Elko with Jerry. It was 120 miles away and I would need a vehicle to bring him home, right? Remember: I am pragmatic. So, I drove to the hospital that day. HAHA Funny to think now that all would be fixed and he would be coming back with me.

After tests and x-rays and head scratching, the decision by the docs in Elko was to move Jerry again by air ambulance to Reno. So, off he went by ambulance to the airport. He was very happy that he would be in yet another ambulance airplane. Jerry himself was a pilot and an A&P, an airframe and power plant mechanic—someone licensed to work on helicopters and airplanes—and loved flying. He graduated second in his class from Northrup Institute of Technology and was always into airplanes and all things flying. So each time he was flown in ambulance planes, he wanted to be the pilot. Anyway, from Elko to Reno, off he went into the wild blue yonder, to bigger, better facilities where he would meet doctors who could fix him up. But I had to get there too. By ground, of course.

I drove back to Eureka, 120 miles, without my other half who was supposed to be coming home with me. Because we were running a small business in a small town on a skinny shoestring budget, we never hired anyone to do things we did ourselves—like bookkeeping and payroll. When I got to the store that afternoon, I gathered up accounts receivables to send out the end-of-the-month bills while in Reno; I also needed to do payroll. Late that afternoon, I drove to Reno, another 242 miles. All in one day. A day that would not be the longest day in the journey ahead of us.

When I walked into his room at around 9:30 p.m. in what was then Washoe Medical Center and is now Renown Hospital in Reno, Nevada, he looked at me and the first thing he said was, "I'm so sorry." He didn't care what was happening to him. He was more concerned for what this stupid twinge in his back was doing to me.

That in a nut shell was Jerry Machacek.

The prognosis of spinal stenosis is as varied and as unpredictable as a herd of barn cats. And as hard to keep track of as trying to herd those same cats into one place. Spinal stenosis, in short, is when the bone keeps growing inside of the spinal canal, causing pressure on the spinal nerve. Some say it is a condition that just happens; others say it is hereditary. Either way you look at it, his bone grew in his spinal canal until it ran out of room to grow freely and that, in turn, caused the first twinge. And led to the first of what I think was about 18, maybe 19, back surgeries over the next 18 years. It was a ride that included hospitals, rehab stays, doctors, long trips, and an introduction to a lovely pain medicine that was new and just coming into its own in the late 1990s and early 2000s—OxyContin.

I was married to a man who was stronger than OxyContin. We talked a lot over the years as the growth of the pain medication epidemic developed. Quietly and alone, just the two of us, as the terrible sweep of overdoses swelled around us and the nation. That was one thing that really did not come into play for us, a full-blown addiction. Thank you, Jesus. As close to the beginning of the drug's inception as we were and as long as he was taking Oxy, Percocet, Fentanyl, Valium, and a nerve medication called Neurontin, along with all the diabetes medications and insulin, we were lucky. We were always open and talked to each other. This openness was our saving grace where the pain medication was concerned and was in a constant swirl around us.

We saw a lot along the way concerning the drugs he was taking for pain. Oh, and there was *a lot* of pain and pain medication. We finally noticed this. There are two types of personalities—addictive and non-addictive. Sounds too simple, doesn't it?

I was lucky to be married to a man with a non-addictive personality. I have no other explanation for the way he took the pain, the heartbreak of another surgery, and another round of new symptoms. He just never, thank the good Lord, *never* took more medicine to become what you would think would be addicted. Oh, his body most certainly was addicted. Come on, I dealt with a lot over those years not to see what the chemicals did to the body. His mind, though, never was. From Percocet and OxyContin, all the way to Fentanyl Patches and other such goodies. More pain and stronger medicines. That was truly something unbelievably amazing for us both. His strength.

But diabetes was waiting, growing inside of him. Diabetes is known as the silent killer. I now know that to be true.

Well, as luck would have it, during all of Jerry's surgeries and stays at rehabilitation hospitals to regain strength and mobility, I also encountered a medical problem of my own. Great.

While waiting in the oh so comfy hospital waiting room chairs during one of Jerry's extensive surgeries, in which doctors opened my husband's back an amazing 19 inches to do repairs, I felt my right foot go to sleep. When I got up to walk, it wouldn't move and I nearly fell. You know when you stand and your foot is asleep, so you wiggle it and wait for the pins and needles to start and then the feeling come back?

Well, I waited.

And waited.

The pins and needles didn't come, so I took off like nothing was wrong. It was a long sit after all and I was nearly 50 years old. Maybe that was just how it was in people nearing 50. See, we always make excuses for things we do not understand or have no time to worry about. I think women do that more than men. But it is in nearly all of our DNA, this take-care-of-it-later mentality. Sometimes, though, later can be too late, or never at all.

I walked out of the waiting room and down a long, empty hall. I heard this noise following me. It was a *slap, slap, slap* as I walked. I stopped and turned around sheepishly to see who was following me. There was nobody there. So, I went on.

Slap, slap, slap.

Must be an echo on the walls, so I went about my business. Off to the new room in the Neuro Ward where my new-and-once-again patient and I would spend the next week.

Slap, slap, slap.

After a week in the hospital, Jerry was moved to a wonderful rehabilitation center. It was in that rehabilitation hospital that a physical therapist noticed the *slap, slap, slap* of whatever was following me. She said I had something called a "dropped foot." Well, what the good gravy Marie was that all about?

Here are the cliff notes.

When Jerry was finally discharged from rehabilitation, we went to one last checkup appointment with his neurosurgeon before we left Reno. A wonderful man who, by this time, I was on a first-name basis with. He would laugh and shake his head when he saw us coming. Well, while at that appointment, Jerry couldn't keep his mouth shut about my foot.

The doctor said, "Hop up on the table and let me take a look."

Oh, great, right?

Well, sure enough, he said I had a "dropped foot" and that he could fix it. After a month or so, he did fix my silly foot—with my very own back surgery. How lucky for me. I must toot my own horn here however.

After any surgery, the patient is hooked up to what is called a PCA (patient-controlled analgesia). A PCA is a type of pain management system that lets you, the patient who is lying in bed after a "procedure," decide when to receive a dose of pain medicine. *Wahoo!* The patient is given a red button to push when the pain is great enough; a shot of pain medicine, usually morphine, is administered via I.V. You know, the good stuff…

I am here to tell you I never pushed that button. Even the nurses couldn't believe I never took pain meds. I think they still talk about the woman who never used her PCA after back surgery! I credit our neurosurgeon Dr. Jay Morgan with Sierra

Neurosurgery. He was and still is a great surgeon and a friend who, don't get me wrong, I hope I never see again…

So, my foot got fixed. Overnight in the hospital and back home and back to work a day later. But the doctor just couldn't leave it alone. Why had I gotten the dropsies in the first place? Off to tests! I even got my very *own* neurologist. Blah, blah, blah and about seven or eight months later, I am standing in a storage shed out back of the hardware store in the middle of a very cold March talking to my loveable neuro guy, Dr. Timothy Louie, on the phone. After listening to him hmm and haw, I finally said, "Just let me have it. Do I have MS or not?"

It got very quiet as I don't think he even thought I knew what I had. He said, "Well, I don't usually do a diagnosis this way. But yes, you have MS." All I could do was laugh. It was just one more thing to pile on top. It was "A Thingy." Today I still call it "A Thingy." Yes, my Multiple Sclerosis is just "A Thingy."

I mean, come on. What are you going to do with a diagnosis like that? I am not a fall-into-a-puddle kind of gal. I had too much on my plate, a plate that was getting smaller but fuller all the time. If there was… No, wait.

There *was* a blessing to this.

Yes, it was MS. I will have it forever. But—please do not think I am poo-pooing all things MS is and can do—as bad as MS can get, I am blessed with what I call MS lite (knock on wood). It affects me in wonderful ways. Ways that have slowed me down. I think that was His plan all along. Slow down and enjoy life a titch, Trina.

The days swam into each other. The weeks, months, and those last years which were always busy and hard and stressful could have been so much worse had I not been diagnosed with MS when I was. I learned to stop when I was tired. I learned to let a lot of crap that I would have taken to heart fall away. Some stuff just had to take a far back seat. I decided, I could, in some small ways, make life better for Jerry. That became my mission. To make his life as good as it could be as he slipped away—and nobody but he and I knew it was happening in those last years. Because we worked together to see it happened just that way.

Okay, so now you know the back story of how we got to the last leg of his life. It was between Thanksgiving and Christmas of 2017 when he caught a cold.

Over time, we realized he wasn't getting better. Wasn't shaking that dang cold. I said, "Come on, Jer. Let me take you to the clinic in town." He said after Christmas he would go if he didn't feel better. In those few short days, he became dependent on me. More so than in all the years he was sick. Over all the years we were in business, we acquired some medical equipment, one of which was an oxygen concentrator. A big, loud brown machine that took oxygen out of the air and concentrated it into tubes that you then put in your nose to get more air. He never needed oxygen before; a few days into the cold, I had to bring this old machine in. He was more comfortable but still saying, "Let's wait and see." Then, after Christmas, he said, "Let's wait 'til after the New Year holiday."

On January 2, I said, "Enough is enough." The concentrator could only produce about five liters of O2; it wasn't enough to keep him from huffing and puffing.

Now, we've always been self-sufficient; we're not ones to ask for help. For us to use the concentrator without a doctor or medical professional or to do any other medical stuff without permission was par for the course for us. We had both taken classes to become CNAs (Certified Nurse Assistants) and knew a bit about taking care of each other. That wasn't something new to us or to the hardy people who lived in our neck of the woods. It was the way of things—if something went wrong, you tended to it yourself, until you couldn't.

It was at that point, January 2, 2018, that I hauled him into the clinic in Eureka.

After poking and prodding, hooking him up to 15 liters of oxygen, and him still huffing to get a full deep breath, no way to draw blood and get results back for at least 24 hours, and more this-ing and that-ing and some hushed hallway discussions, the PA (physician's assistant) on staff asked me what I thought. This was not out of the norm either. Jerry was a strong man who just wanted a shot of something in his butt and then to go home and get better. The rest of us buzzing around him could see he was sicker than even he was aware.

In the end, I said, "Call the airplane. Let's get him to Elko." That really was the only option.

Was it wrong? Did I make the right decision that day?

For a long, long time, I've wondered and second-guessed that decision, and the tons of others that I made over the following nine days.

Off to the airport in yet another ambulance he went. As per my usual routine, I followed the ambulance out to the airport in my truck. It was a conglomeration of errors that day. I should have seen the writing on the wall when the airplane landed at our tiny but wonderful Eureka airport and it was relayed to us waiting in the ambulance on the tarmac that the pilot had found something wrong with the airplane. So that wonderful air ambulance was grounded and a second plane was called out. But it would be about an hour or more before it arrived. Everyone was very nice and patient and couldn't do enough for us.

At Elko, it was discovered that Jerry had some new-to-us heart issues, so he was stuffed into the Cath Lab. The personnel there found out he had a blockage, but it wasn't anything to worry about until whatever else was going on could be addressed, the cardiologist told me.

Okay, so it wasn't the heart. Good.

Along this path, the doctors also addressed the enormous amounts of water he was retaining. Next came the pills to—well, in the nicest of terms—force the water from his body. Gallons and gallons of water. Now, this took place over a few days, not in one big event. So, eventually, wonderful people came to see him; he loved to visit. Jerry was feeling better and began sitting up again. He chatted from the edge of his bed with the pastor of our church about the project they were working on to build a new Eureka Community Church. Everything was looking up.

Then, around the fourth day in the hospital, he got kind of quiet. Really quiet. A doctor pulled me aside to explain that Jerry wasn't expelling potassium and that his heart was getting dangerously close to stopping because of that build up.

What?

"Well, let's get right on top of taking care of that," I told him.

Again, blah, blah, blah. A day or so goes by and this potassium-thingy was addressed with a machine which forces air into you and then sucks it out at a high pressure, somehow withdrawing potassium from your system. Well, the pressure was set so high that when Jerry was hooked up, it scared the crap out of him and he pulled it off (no, he ripped it off and threw it across the room). He refused to put it back on.

You know, through all those years of doctors, surgeries, rehabilitations, epidural shots, medicines, ambulances and plane rides, and long road trips to and from doctors and tests and all the pain—so much pain—that was the one and only time he got pissed off and declined treatment. It was an awful thing. Just awful. And if I could have gotten hold of the technician who had set that machine up, I would have thrown her out the window.

Whew, I feel better.

As an aside, it is okay to say what is on your mind. Oh, it takes time and practice. If you hold it in, you'll not literally explode, but that pent-up anger and frustration will show up at the most unexpected times. You cry when you do not want to. You might kick a tree and break a toe and really, what did that tree ever do to you? **So, give yourself permission to get mad— then, move on.** Staying mad is counterproductive. There is still a lot of living to do. Yes, you will have a lot of life after a death.

Potassium buildup within the body is, obviously, not a good thing. Without intervention, the potassium increases until heart muscles seize. Because the heart is a muscle, the potassium basically causes it to cramp which, you know, is a heart attack. So, what would happen if Jerry's potassium level was not addressed?

Well, at the time, it wasn't *if* but *when* that happened, the next step was to intubate and draw the potassium off while he was in a coma-like state. Once finished, he would be brought back around and all would be right with the world. Ta-da! That was the plan—until diabetes finally decided to stand up and be counted.

A day here and a day there to talk and wait and see, or just wait. Jerry would be there then not as he went in and out of consciousness. He would talk like he was on top of the world to a visitor before falling asleep for 20 hours as I sat and sang little made-up songs and read to him from the Bible.

He was calm and we talked, but we didn't, I am ashamed to say, *talk* like we should have. There was one point when he asked me what was going on and I told him he was pretty sick. In typical Jerry fashion, he couldn't believe that he was so sick. I remember him just rolling over in bed and saying, "No way."

Later, when the room was full of doctors, a social worker, and a nurse and everyone was talking simultaneously, he just looked to me for an explanation. I told him the plan—because he refused to use that sucking air machine, we were going to wait until his heart stopped, then take all the steps to draw the potassium off. I looked at him point-blank and asked if that was what he wanted; he nodded. So, that was the plan. Let him slip into a coma and bring him back when he was better. Ha, yeah. Great plan.

You know, it took three days for that to happen. It was so stressful. It was so awful. But! But as awful as it all was, it was so wonderful to spend time with him, even at the end. When he knew I was there. Oh, *he knew*. And I know he knew. Of course, that wasn't supposed to be the *real* end.

When I looked back some time after it all was over, I never thought, not for one split second, that Jerry would not be coming home with me that January. We had been through so much in all our 41 years, 8 months, and 1 day. He would just get medicine and we would come home.

Oh, but it ended though, didn't it? Not only did his heart stop, but that diabetes-thing forced his kidneys and lungs to quit. And on January 11 at 2:30 p.m., just as I finished reading the 23rd

Psalm and the Lord's Prayer to him, his face—which had been in such a terrible state of pain for so many years, his body which had been through so much for so many years—seemed to relax and let go.

Then, the strongest man I have ever known breathed his last breath. I kissed him as he and I separated from this life. He zipped to Heaven in one quiet, last whoosh of air... You could not have scripted a more peaceful ending to an amazing life. A life so very full to nearly overflowing with the effervescence of life itself. He was 73 and I was 62.

And I was relieved.

And yes, I felt the guilt of relief.

And yes, I still do.

5

The Mortuary, Oh Swell

There are several things I have wanted to be in my life. Rich and famous notwithstanding, I have also wanted to be a really good waitress and a bush pilot. Oh, and thin. I have always wanted to be thin. So far, I have attained only one of those—that waitress-thingy. When I was young. And I was a really good waitress.

I have not, however, in any way, shape, or form wanted to be a policewoman or a mortician. But I am so very glad there are people who have taken up the staff to fill those important and under-appreciated slots in life. I have known many cops. Uh, as friends and not in their official capacities, thank you very much! But I have never known anyone from the mortician side of life. My husband had an uncle who was a mortician. He was in on the hubbub of burying media magnate William Randolph Hearst. He was even featured in a picture in *Life Magazine* during the Hearst procession. Weird how I thought of that now…

Your mind can take you to places at times that will seem out of the norm. Might put you off balance. I told myself it was my mind trying to adjust to the trials, tests, and bumps encountered in those first days and weeks. Trust me—you are *not* losing your sanity. You are just, as your car may tell you when you get off your route, "recalculating." You are allowed to wander. It's one of the perks, if there are perks, of becoming a widow.

Nobody I know gets up in the morning and thinks, *Wow. I'll just pop on over to the mortuary and see what's going on.* Nobody. So, when I woke up and realized a visit to the mortuary was on my list, I wanted to pull the covers back up over my head and never come out. As I think back, I still feel that dread, that sick-to-the-pit-of-my-gut feeling. Of course, I handled it with all the calm, cool, grown-up finesse I could muster. And humor.

The day after Jerry's death, I found myself sitting in a funeral home, also known as the mortuary—I call it the "dead-guy place."

I really hoped something, anything, would magically transport me out of there, out of that weird, scary place where, in what I perceived to be a dark and cold room of that funny-smelling place, my husband's body waited to be cremated.

There is only one dead-guy place in Elko. I was lucky to have my brother and sister-in-law with me for those last hours of Jerry's life and the following miserable days. So, when I went to the dead-guy place, my brother, Rod, went with me.

Now, going to the dead-guy place is scary. If you aren't scared, you are tougher than me. I applaud you for your toughness, for sure. But if you are like the rest of us mere mortals, you will be nervous; let that be your defense. Because this is your first huge duty as a new widow, remember the following: keep your head about you; don't overspend; and for goodness' sake, keep your virtual bag of smiles nearby. You will need them. In fact, you will find yourself pulling out that sack of smiles several times in the days ahead. **It really is okay to smile again.**

Upon approaching the front door of the mortuary, I noticed a door bell which we were encouraged to ring to enter. I thought—and still do think—that was very strange. But! In ringing the doorbell, I was transported to another time when Jerry and I were installing a wrought-iron fence that we—well, mostly Jerry—built to corral the family plot at the Cedar Hills Cemetery, one of several around Eureka where the Machaceks are marked with impressive pieces of granite and marble. Jerry's handiwork was, as usual, impressive. He made a wonderfully ornate fence with a gate boasting a decorative latch that was so perfectly level it closed with ease. Jerry and I laughed when I asked, "You trying to keep people out or people in?" Yes, at the cemetery we laughed.

26

While waiting for someone to answer the doorbell at the dead-guy place, I could hear Jerry's laugh as I implied he was trying to keep the living and the dead in their respective areas. The times of our lives—when we were younger, healthier, and both alive.

This mortuary stuff is a business; as such, they provide a service to the public while attempting to make a living and, yes, a profit. They have seen people at the very worst of times. So dealing with you, they should show compassion and be helpful. But it is a business. They are there to sell their services and products. Even though this will be one of the toughest things that will smack you in the face, keep your head.

Eventually, the front door was unlocked. Inside, we were escorted down a hallway past the showroom of caskets to a room where we were told to wait. I sat, feeling kinda stupid and off center. As Rod and I looked at each other, I thought, *Well, this isn't how I want to spend my day!* Looking back, I'm sure my big brother was thinking the same thing. I was thankful he was there, even if the look on his face said he would rather be someplace, any place, else. I thought, *me too.*

It was *so* quiet. So quiet you could hear one of those caskets drop! HAHA See, laughter really *is* the best medicine. Then, enter the mortician, aka the dead-guy place guy. He was soft-spoken, nice, and understanding. We sat at a large conference table and all things involved were dealt with.

You might be one of the people who may have made prearrangements on your own or with a loved one. If that is the case, some of what will happen you will have dealt with. But know that there will still be tasks left to complete to "finish" your job as the one left behind.

As I have said, Death is sudden, expected, or unexpected. But this first big step will bring you to a door of closure that you will be set in front of many times in the coming days, weeks, months, and years. Put on that grown-up face of yours. **You're going to be a mess, but over time, you will heal** and hopefully be able to help someone else struggling to make it through day one.

We went over the costs of cremation because Jerry and I had decided on that when we were doing our wills so very long ago.

Wait. What? You have no will? Your road will be harder than you can imagine. Tell everyone you know—**write a will!** Just saying.

Anyway, talking with the dead-guy guy and blah, blah, blah this and hooptie-do that, I finally got out my checkbook. As I was writing the check to pay for this guy to turn "the body" into ashes, I tapped my pen on the table and looked the guy right in the eye and said, "Now, you make dang-sure he is dead before you light that fire!"

Oh, the look on his face! Priceless...

I know, I know. It was quite irreverent of me. But that is how I handled it. **How you go about it will be your way.** If you go with your kids, if you go with your family, if you go with a friend, try to keep your head about you. As hard as it is. Think. Think. *Think.* This is not the time to try to keep up with the Joneses and spend more than you can afford. Remember, you are the one left behind, and you are still alive; you are in charge of every aspect of mortuary and funeral things. There will be plenty of people around you with their thoughts and ideas. Be open, respectful, loving, and caring—but be smart. Be you, the best you can be. Cry, laugh, be a mess, just be focused. Just be careful with your heart and your checkbook.

Funerals are for those left behind. As a Christian, I know that by the time the funeral or services are offered, He will have already received the loved one in His arms. I like to say, and I really believe this, I was happier for Jerry that he went to his glory than I was sad for me to be left behind. **So do what you feel comfortable with and let everything else just fall away.** It will be okay. Don't second-guess yourself; there is no right or wrong here. No rules or regulations. **Just make a decision or choice and move on.** Good, bad, or indifferent, you are in charge.

Oh yeah, and order extra death certificates.

Yes, they are something that you get charged for. Figure out what you might need and then order extras. You will need them for a weird array of things. Including life insurance. It seems that anyone or any business that has to do with money or finances will always want a "certified" death certificate. That is to say, they will not take a copy; they want one with a raised seal to fill some slot they will have to prove to someone in their office or in some far-off department that your loved one really did die and you really have the right to be the one left behind to do all the cleanup work. That you really do have rights to *everything* you are telling them you have the rights to.

You will need that very important paper for the bank and, for some reason, utility companies. Department of Motor Vehicles will want one of their very own if you need to change titles of cars, trailers, and the like. Any other government office you might have dealings with will also want their very own certificate. So, when I say order more than you think you will need, I am not just blowing smoke at you. Order extras. You will never be any closer to someone who can get you these important papers than the guy you are buying a funeral from. Isn't that wonderful?

Be ready for this too. **It is hard to look at a death certificate.** Crazy because it's just a piece of paper. How many pieces of paper have you held in your hands over the course of your life? I don't know. Maybe holding that stupid but super important document makes it feel more official. Maybe seeing those "cause of death" or "date of death" boxes filled out just feels so permanent. **Whatever it is, be ready. It's another first.** Another step. Another piece of the puzzle you're putting together to create your new life.

If your loved one was in the military, there will be a wonderful surprise of a governmental death benefit. As of today, it is $250.00. Which the mortuary will credit you on the final tabulation of your bill; they will do all the paperwork to get that amount from the government for you—and them. Also, if it fits your situation, you will be entitled to a United States flag. The mortuary should offer one to you. If they don't, be sure to ask for it. It is something your loved one fought for and as a lasting memorial and as the one left behind, it is a last "Thank You" from our country. So, ask! You might also be given one from your local VFW group.

Setting everything up with the mortuary will not be pleasant. It will be hard. **If you feel yourself slipping away, stop, rest, and eat something.**

Then Sweet Pea, gather yourself up and keep going. Because your life is just beginning. Your after-a-death life is going to be something you can't even imagine. Yet. Believe it or not (I know you can't believe it quite yet), you are going to have some amazing times ahead. Keep going.

This is the first column I wrote and disseminated after Jerry died. This "Is This You?" dang near wrote itself. I like to think Jerry would have approved. It was as hard as it was easy to write. It was so well-received that I thought here in this spot, at this time, it would be fitting. It posted in newspapers the week of January 14, 2018.

Is This You?

Lost and Found

Yesterday, January 11th, my husband, my other half for nearly 42 years, passed away. Now, I tell you that not for you to be sad for me, although I am sad enough for me, you, and anyone else you can see, hear, or think of. But to rejoice in the knowledge that he is now in what I feel is such a wonderful place. And since over the years "Is This You?" has typically been a giggle fest, you probably already know that I will keep this light even though it deals with the death of my loved one...

When someone is gone forever from your life, it is referred to as a loss. But it is not like the loss of that one sock somewhere in the washing machine one-lost-sock twilight zone. I have thought of this for the past week. He isn't lost, I know exactly where he is, and I rejoice in knowing that. But! I figure it's called a loss because there really is no other word for it. I mean, if you check a thesaurus, under "loss" you can find alternatives. But you wouldn't say, "Sorry for your deficit" or "Sorry for your defeat." I should like to think that I am just sorry to be alone.

So, as irreverent as you may see it, here are some "tales out of school" that have happened in the past few days that I have used to keep my sanity and to keep the faces of those around me from looking at me with such fear that they will say the wrong thing—because as I see it, there is no "wrong" thing to say when you are trying to comfort a soul who is now alone.

First thing I think of is this... At the same time we entered the hospital and found it a real possibility that I would be leaving *alone*, my other half had a very good friend of 60-plus years in another hospital fighting for his life. We talked about how strange it was that the two of them had gone through so much together over the years. Their biggest thing was building cars, and when they were young, they drove fast and raced those cars— a lot. So, in my special way to keep things light, I asked my other half what he thought he was doing being sick. Were he and his friend racing to the grave? He laughed. His friend is not out of the woods, but he is still fighting the good fight. So, ta-da! Look at who won this race!

At one point, there was some hallucinations going on with my other half. Looking out the window, he said to me, "Turn around and look at the Eskimos outside on the roof!" It lasted for just a few seconds then the confusion was gone and he knew there were no Eskimos outside on the roof! I asked him if he knew where the Eskimos went. He knew what was coming, laughed, shook his head, and retold me the little poem I had made up about squirrels over the years. But he put in Eskimos instead of squirrels. (Trust me, the following is in no way meant as disrespect to Eskimos who are a grand people.) "The Eskimos were in their little Eskimo houses in their little Eskimo beds and had pulled their little Eskimo blankets up over their little Eskimo heads." Even though we kinda knew that we—well, he—was fighting what we Christians call the last fight, he remained a funny guy and he was using *my* line doing it!

We talked several times over the years and decided that we would both be cremated at the end of our time on Mother Earth. Off-handedly, you say you will be cremated and it slides off your shoulder like melting butter. But in my mind, and maybe yours too, you get to wondering, *What if there is just a hint of life in me when the oven goes whoosh?*

So, at the mortuary after all was said and done, as I was talking to the gentleman who had helped me through *this* last door of the whole process, I looked him in the eye and said without flinching, "Now, you be sure he is really gone before you light that torch, okay?"

Oh my, you could have heard a coffin drop! I know, really, really know, that I heard my other half laugh. It was at that moment that even though I have, am, and will forever be a bit *lost*, my other half *found* Glory, Home, and Peace.

Oh, and he is fishing all the time!

What else could I want for him?

6

What Then Remains?

Well, well, well. If you are here, you have made it through the mortuary stuff. See, you are stronger than you ever thought you would be. Congrats!

I would, however, be remiss if I didn't touch on my last trip to the dead-guy place—to pick up the ashes. Now, if you are having a funeral, you will not have to deal with this. You might want to skip this part of my story, but you won't. Human nature dictates that most people want to learn every little thing that happens in someone else's life to better prepare themselves. So, here is what happened when I traveled to pick up what was left of the man with whom I lived for 42 years, 8 months, and 1 day.

Firstly, it was a long drive, approximately 120 miles. Now, that isn't a big thing to me. I am used to going 120 miles for groceries, the doctor, and the nearest Burger King or Wendy's. It's true, you know. That saying, "Location. Location. Location." Well, my location is 120 miles from the nearest everything.

I got the call about a week after handling all the dealings with the mortuary. By that time, I was alone in my home. My family had returned home—because they had their own lives and jobs to deal with—and I was now left to fend for myself. I knew my life was not their responsibility. I was as ready for them to leave as much as they were ready to leave. Of course, they'd return for the services, but before all that, the ashes had to be retrieved. That was my thing that needed to be done alone. I needed to face up and do it.

The morning after I got the call from the mortuary, I got cleaned up and dressed. My stomach fluttered as I didn't know what the day would bring much less what I was about to do. I thought it was because of where I was going. But it wasn't. It was because I was going to go out on the road—by myself.

This first was a tear jerker.

I got all the way out to the garage and into the car. Even put the key in the ignition and started the car. I looked over at the passenger seat, and nobody was there. I was in the car without my copilot. It was the weirdest feeling. I had driven all over the state alone to hospitals, from hospitals, following airplanes and ambulances.

I mean, for the past two weeks, I had traveled to and from the hospital by myself. Drove myself home that 120 miles with my brother and sister-in-law right behind me in their vehicle. Drove into my yard by myself for the first time. Drove into that garage by myself. Walked into my home by myself, knowing he would never again be there. So many firsts were happening so fast. Not to mention going to bed in our bed truly alone for the first time. During the past ten or so years, I had done more and more things by myself as he had gotten sicker; things had gradually been turned over to me. What was the big deal about this little 120-mile jaunt back to the mortuary?

Well, for starters, I would always be without my copilot now. I grabbed hold of the steering wheel and just sat there. I tried to buck myself up by sitting a little higher in the seat. Tossed my hair back, looked at myself in the rearview mirror. Oh yes, I looked like crap. Even pinched my cheeks like an old lady trying to put some color in my silly face. I told myself that this was just a step. It was no big thing to go by myself. Just another step.

It hit me right then and there that I was truly in charge of me. Nobody around to check if it was time to go. Nobody around to make sure I had my purse, money, directions, and lists and that the car was gassed up. All those things I had already been doing for many years, but now? Now, it truly was up to me. So as my knuckles grew whiter on the steering wheel, I sat there and cried. For me. I cried for me.

Metaphorically, I think I grew up right there. I pushed the button to raise the garage door, backed out, and headed down the road—to go and pick up those ashes. I think about that day a lot. I was amazed when sometime later, like a few years later, I mentioned it to a friend who had recently lost her husband. To my amazement, she had experienced the same feelings the first time she got in her car to go somewhere. Truly by herself. She lived in a city, so it wasn't the miles traveled, just the travel, the act of going that we both dealt with. It was something so unexpected. That told me I was not the first to deal with those emotions, nor would I be the last.

So, I'll be there for you, and you will be there for someone, and they will do the same. It's a club nobody wants to be invited into, but since we're there, helping hands are good hands.

I pulled onto the highway and turned up the radio as loud as I could stand. HAHA Once I got going, it actually was not as bad as I thought it was going to be while I had been sitting in the garage sniveling. It was sunny but cold, and thankfully, even though it was January, the roads were clear. The miles clicked by like they had so many times before. Then I got to the mortuary. I didn't really feel dread; I think I was just numb. Numbness against the cold reality is a blessing. That numbness will last for a while. Trust me: you will want that numbness to last for as long as possible. It is an insulator that I all-too-soon realized I wanted to last. I was still in the numbness stage as I rang the doorbell at the dead-guy place. Isn't that just wrong on so many levels?

While making arrangements there a few days prior, I thought of something Jerry had once said to me—that it would be interesting to see all the hardware the doctors put into his back and neck over the years. He had mentioned more than once that it would be fascinating to see what all was in there. At the time, we had had a good laugh because we both know when Death came, he wouldn't be around to observe the screws and plates because, you know, he wouldn't be there. Kinda ghoulish, right?

Soon, I found myself standing in a little room, waiting for what I knew would be a white box in which would be my husband. Oh, I was *so* very out of my comfort zone.

Pretty soon, in walked the dead-guy place guy with not one but *two* white boxes. Like, gift boxes. One was big, about the size of a personal watermelon, but square. On top of that box was a littler white one. About the size of a baked potato. He handed them to me after I signed the paper, swearing I was who I was. Oh, and he gave me the flag too.

When I had previously gone with Jerry to pick up his mother's remains, we had only been given one box. Here, I must have hit the lottery because I got *two*! Me being me, I asked, "Uh, why are there two boxes?" I mean my husband was a big man. He was always a big guy. But two boxes? The guy very respectfully explained that the second box held the hardware I had asked for. And a chill went up and down my spine. I know I heard Jerry say to me, "Cool!"

I left with my two boxes, a flag, and my dignity. Got into my car, put my boxes and flag on the passenger seat, and with my copilot where he should be, I headed for home. Taking him home for the last time.

7

In Memoriam

O h, the lovingly orchestrated service. In a world of firsts that comes chugging along after the death of someone, hopefully this goodie will not only be a "first" but an "only" event.

There are so many ways to title a funeral. Some call it a memorial. Like I did. I held a memorial service for Jerry. Somewhat new to me is a Celebration of Life. While a funeral is geared toward the orderly and spiritual or church type of event, a celebration of life is more relaxed and in tune with the telling of stories of the life of the one who passed away, possibly without any church stuff. A service can be either a funeral or a memorial. Both of these, while they may or may not be in a church, will have some spiritual aspects. The big difference is that a memorial service is done without a body; a funeral service is held when there is a body that will be buried.

I chose a memorial service because there were a few things I didn't want to have done. Like pick out the clothes my significant other would be buried in, or how his hair will be combed. Or whether to have an open or closed casket. I admire anyone who has to make those decisions. I am thankful we discussed our last wishes over the years of our lives. Didn't really think I would ever be in the position to carry them all out though. No, the decisions I made in regards to the memorial service were hard enough.

As crazy as it sounds, my biggest fear in having any kind of service was that I would put it all together, and nobody would be there. I dreaded sitting in a big open hall and turning around to find dozens of empty chairs. It was as real to me as you sitting there reading these words. And I couldn't shake it.

It wasn't until a few months later that I figured out why I had felt that way. It was because as our lives had moved along, he had been the driving force while I had been in the background doing the outskirt work. He was the barker of the circus of our life, and I was the one who made sure the curtain went up and down. You know, the one who picked up after the elephants went through. HEE HEE HEE. Oh, people *knew* who I was; of course, they did. In my mind's eye, I was Jerry's wife. Not Trina, just Jerry's wife. I thought that if I, Jerry's wife, was to have a service, who would come? It was, as I see it now, one of the mind tricks that bounced around in my head during the mourning process.

At the memorial service, people started to file in. My crew around me told me the church would not be big enough. I had my doubts but went with the majority on the place to hold the service. We held it in the Eureka Opera House, a wonderful building my husband and I helped transfer from private hands to Eureka County's ownership through the historical society. Beautifully refurbished to its original nineteenth-century glory, it was perfect.

When I finally sat for the service to begin, I sneaked a peek around. The place was full to standing room capacity; there were even people in the balcony. And as such the girl I am, of course I cried. It wasn't that I was crying for me. I was crying that Jerry couldn't be there to see how many people had come to say good-bye to him. And as it turned out—to say hello to me. I was dumbfounded.

It was a pleasant surprise to learn that people knew who I was. They were just waiting for me to come out from his shadow to be the person I am today. It was an amazing, sadly happy day, one that I will cherish forever.

I am on a journey, learning more about myself each and every day. Turns out that is the good side of widowhood. Finding yourself and liking what you find.

Things will happen so fast in those few days and weeks after your loved one dies that you will definitely feel overwhelmed. Just remember, do all the things you need to do: **stop, rest, and eat!** That is the best advice I can give you. I will give it to you more than once. **Stop, rest, and eat!**

Between myself, a few friends, my brother, and sister-in-law, we picked the date, the place, and the time. When someone asks, "What about pictures," the floodgates open.

What about programs?
What about flowers?
What about thank-you cards?
What about an obituary submission to the local paper?
What about posting memorial service information in stores and locations in and around town?

I wrote his obituary myself. Come on, I *am* a writer! It was the best, hardest, and easiest thing for me to write. I did it when I was alone and just let my fingers put into words what my heart felt.

The obituary is something that needs to be done in a fairly timely manner. It is not only a short telling of a life well lived but a way to announce a death, to let people know about services, and whether you will be receiving donations. Mostly, I took it as a way to release some of the feelings I had and wanted to express to his friends that he was a man who lived a full life... And then he left me behind, the little stinker.

Yes, of course, it is all about me! It's okay, you know, to say everything you do is all about you. It took a while, but I finally realized that he was the one who died, not me. So yes, it sometimes is *all about me*. In all facets of my life, I am the only one who is in charge of me, as hard as it sometimes is to say.

It will be all about you and your life too. Remember: what you do from here on out will define you. Define you the way you want to. **Your life really is all about you!**

Family and friends were my best asset. Things got done in orderly chaos. A great example is this. We were members of the Gideon Ministry. You may know the Gideons as the angels who place Bibles in hotels and motels. I notified the president of our local group and he put out the word to the members. They showed up in droves and even picked up flowers that were sent from Jerry's surgeon in Reno to a florist in a town 120 miles away. We don't have a florist in Eureka, so flowers had to be ordered and brought in by family and friends.

My sister-in-law Julie took over the task of getting the programs and thank-you cards printed and so much more. She picked up flowers that I ordered for the service from another town 80 miles away. She did so much that I am sure I will not ever be able to thank her enough. She, my brother, and their children are my only family. When Jerry was dying, my nephew Damon, dropped everything and drove from Reno to Elko to be with me until Rod and Julie could get there as they were traveling up from Yuma where they were snow birding the winter away. The three of them were rocks I could cling to. Rod, as hard as it was for him to be the center of attention, led the service and introduced speakers. It was one of the very few times I saw my big brother cry.

The service itself was cool. We had prayers, a bit of a eulogy, some laughter and tears as we opened the service for people to speak their hearts of Jerry and how his life intertwined with others. We had music that he loved. It wasn't long. It wasn't staunch. It wasn't suits and ties; it was down to earth. My wonder-filled niece Marci put together a collage of pictures and a music video that played before and after the "service." She loved her Uncle Jerry, and it showed in what she did for him—and me. It was what he would have enjoyed. It was also what I enjoyed. To this day, I think funerals and the like are for those left behind. That day was no exception; it was for the living, not for the dead.

Jerry was an only child and his parents had already passed away, so his family was in short supply. Some of his cousins came, and it was wonderful to hear them talk about how Jerry fit into their lives. Ah, the friends from his life were varied and so wonderful to see. I found the service as heartwarming as it was hard.

Men he had known would come up to me and tell me little stories of how Jerry had affected them or how he had made them something in the machine shop. He was a self-taught master machinist, and in all of his life, he never knew the word "no." If someone needed something, he would move heaven and earth to help. That was the Jerry I was being told about over and over during the social time of the service. I needed those conversations so much. I cannot tell you how much I still covet those shared tidbits. Even today, people who knew him tell me things about their connections to Jerry.

It wasn't just Jerry's friends who turned out for this service. Friends of mine were there. I remember seeing a girlfriend I hadn't seen in many years walking into the hall to attend the service. I couldn't believe she had traveled across the state to give me a hug that I can still feel today. That's what I mean when I say services are for the living. Hard as the day was, it was just as rewarding.

I gathered pictures of Jerry and his friends doing all the things they did over the years and attached them to make posters. This was such fun to watch at the service. His friends reliving fishing trips and vacations and hunting and just being alive around Jerry. It was almost as good as the wonderful video Marci created. There were things being done that today that I look back on and think, *How did that happen?* It just did, somehow.

Don't try to micromanage this event. I have a tendency to do that. I am sure I would have been a helicopter mom had I had kids. With time and age comes the knowledge that things will get done the way they are supposed to get done. For instance, I knew, I just *knew*, if I didn't do everything myself, everything wouldn't get done. Kind of full of myself, wasn't I? Well, turns out that more things than I could shake a stick at happened. All without me sticking my finger into each and every pie that was created to pull off the memorial service. Like the food.

Of course, there was the food. I didn't even know there was going to be food because the women who provided it, did it out of true love. In our little community, a potluck dinner was customary. Ladies from a mix of churches became miracle workers, bringing all that together in the background, quietly and without applause. Well, I applauded and appreciated them. They even wrapped stuff up for me to take home. When I said it was just me, they smiled and handed me another bag of rolls or some cake or salad. At the time, I thought I would never use it all. I froze most, and you know what? I was still pulling things out of my freezer months later and heating up dinner. They knew what they were doing, and I bless them to this day for their foresight and kindness. Who knew? Those ladies did, that's who.

The service is anything and everything you can imagine. It won't be perfect. Just like a wedding, perfect or not, there will still be a wedding. Or a funeral. Don't let the fact that it won't be perfect bother you. It will be as perfect as it should be. It will be remembered for a while, and then it will be forgotten. By everyone but you. You will always remember it. You will remember the hugs and the looks and the sights and sounds and the food and laughter and the tears. One thing you will not remember? You won't remember who was *not* there. I say that for two reasons.

First. It is not important to know who was and was not there. You were there, and the memories you shared with those who were there will be in your heart and mind forever. You will go to those memories occasionally, and sometimes it will be happy and sometimes it will be sad. Both in good ways.

Second. I truly believe that any service you choose is for the living. Some people are not comfortable showing feelings when dealing with death. Some people will not be able to attend for a varied list of reasons. Rest assured, those who don't attend, for whatever reason, if they care, they will let you know in their own way. A card, a phone call, a visit after all the hoopla is over. We all have our own ways of dealing with the departed.

Honestly? To this day, I cannot attend a funeral or memorial. A few very good men we knew have gone on to their rewards since my other half-zoomed off. I did not go to those events. I know myself well enough to recognize I am not ready. Yes, I know memorial services are for the families left behind. Yes, I know it is the socially expected thing. But! I am not that big of a person to put myself into situations that I am not ready, willing, or capable of handling. I may never be back to that spot. I have guilt, but my life is not all the way back to being able to do that yet. Like me, you will not remember who was *not* there. And that is okay. They didn't come for their own reasons.

Don't sweat the small stuff. Buck up, stand up, head up, chin up, and keep your eye on the prize of becoming the best dang widow you can be. **Yes, your life will now be all about you.**

8

The Closet, the Drawers, and Under the Bathroom Sink

That first day after I got home from the hospital, after he died (again with those words!), I couldn't get all the medical equipment out of sight and out of my house fast enough. He was sick for a long time, so over the years, there were many changes to our home and lives; so many additions became a part of us. I look back, and I can still see all those things in my living room.

So many items were strategically placed around where his electric lifting recliner chair sat, including the oxygen concentrator—that big, brown thing on wheels that, because we didn't have enough tubing to reach from it to the bathroom, I would unplug and roll into the bathroom so he could catch his breath. There was a table where he had an array of amenities to keep him comfortable. Because he was a mechanical genius in my eyes, he had handcrafted a metal apparatus that attached to his chair which held the phone, a remote for the TV/satellite, and a third remote for the DVD player for easy access to the western movies he loved to watch.

At the end, he had acquired three—yes, three—scooters. Two red and one blue. He was always fiddling with them and buying and changing and charging batteries. He built and attached these cute little tables to them so he could sign papers and read while he waited in doctors' waiting rooms. He even put original chromed metal bulldogs from my grandfathers' fleet of MAC trucks on the front of each. It was fun to see little kids come over and talk to the bulldogs and to him. He loved that.

The two scooters in the house and the one in our van were still waiting. For what? It wasn't like he was ever going to use any of them or the mountain of medical stuff in the house again. The two scooters in the house sat on their own rugs in a spare room—his work and play room—plugged into the wall. Waiting. Well, that wasn't going to happen again, was it?

Anger. Sadness. Confusion.

The leftover medical supplies all played a part.

The day after I got home, I started to clean out all things medical. It wasn't hard. You would think it would have been. I mean, it *should* have felt like I was throwing him out. Throwing out all he was. But it wasn't. It was such a *freeing* experience. I am not ashamed to say I could not get all that crap out of my home fast enough.

The last of it all was the chair, his chair. It appeared forlorn, cold. No extra sheepskin to keep his skin from breaking down. No more extra socks and container setting alongside it, brimming with dressings and meds to keep his feet and legs healthy. No more table with tissues and wet wipes and pill reminders and, and, and...

Just that chair. It too would go. It took a few months, but I finally found someone whose mother needed an electric lift chair, and I sold it to her. Man, was it heavy! I was so glad she brought her 20-something-year-old son over to get it out the front door and onto her truck.

And guess what? I cried as it left the yard.

I still haven't filled that chair space with furniture. Actually—you'll probably get a kick out of this—a cannon has claimed that section of the room. Throughout his life, my other half created wonderful things in his machine shop, including a functioning self-designed and constructed quarter-scale black powder cannon which shoots real one-inch lead balls! I am comforted by the memories that cannon evokes in me.

I remember the day we tested the barrel with a triple load of black powder and he touched it off with an extra-long piece of fuse as we hid behind a stack of railroad ties. The boom that barrel and load of powder made was *amazing*. I still hold onto the memories and those things that make me smile. A cannon, *his* cannon! Who knew, right?

The days melted away and people came and went with the conclusion of the Memorial Service. Prior to Jerry's death, we had a young married couple living in a little house on our property. But, all too soon, they were called away and moved to Virginia. Thereafter, they had a baby girl who we all called Bug. In September 2017, they came to visit us and the friends they had left. Jerry absolutely loved giving that tiny Bug rides on his scooter. Her squeals of delight were infectious.

Jerry died that following January. The young family traveled all the way back to bid farewell. I was so happy to see them.

The day after the services, the young woman asked if there was anything they could help me with before they made for Virginia. I looked right at her and said, "Yes. Let's go in and clean out his side of the closet." She probably thought it was too soon, but she knew I meant it. So, to the closet we went.

There are so many ways this can go—the closet cleaning. I have since told this story and gotten looks of surprise and "how could you?" I don't know why I did it the way I did. I do know that I have never regretted my decisions about stuff.

Stuff is just stuff.

Things are just things.

When we meet in our next forever homes, wherever you think that will be—for me, it will be Heaven if I am good enough—our spirits will rejoice. I endeavor to make the best decisions I possibly can at every given moment in time and then move forward.

While I was in the closet getting ready, my young friend asked if I wanted to put his clothes in bags or boxes to take to any thrift stores. I said, "Nope. Throwing it all away." Bless her. She hid her incredulity.

I got out what I call my Old Lady Cart—a four-wheeled thing I use to bring in groceries from the garage—and began filling it with shirts and pants. I would toss and she would ferry that cart out to our dumpster. Good thing we had one of those huge three-cubic-feet dumpsters in our yard at the time. I tossed and she filled the cart, over and over.

Shoes, ties, suits.

Occasionally, my friend would ask if I was sure. My response was to throw more onto the cart.

Belts, Pendleton shirts, coats, sweaters. Hangers and all.

Then up to the top shelf of the closet where the pants and summer shorts were folded, waiting to be worn again. There were piles of jeans and cargo shorts because, over the years, his illness had made his body change; the sizes were never the same from week to week. They all took their last trip out the door to our dumpster.

As he had gotten sicker and weakness became a reality, Jerry went to sweatpants for ease of living in his world. All went into that little cart—and she just kept rolling it out the door, across the deck, and down the ramp Jerry and I had built together to get his scooter into the house so his life could be lived to the fullest.

I started on my side of the closet. I threw out all the things I knew I would never wear again. Including some frilly lacey things he had given me when we were younger. I threw out a very purple, long dress he made me buy because he liked it. I never wore it and it had cost $129.00. The tags were still attached. I threw it away. We never went anywhere where I could have worn it, and I knew I would never wear it now, so out it went.

Finally, I stopped when I got to his Air Force green shirt bearing his name and all of his other patches. That, I kept. That will always be a part of him and one of my last connections to him.

Oh, there was one more item…

My wedding dress was in a trunk. I looked at it. I wanted to burn it; I wanted to keep it; I wanted it to just disappear. It is still wrapped in plastic from the dry cleaner in my closet. Not hanging. Not folded. Not protected. Just rolled up in that drycleaner plastic sitting on top of his last pillow. Waiting. I'll do something with it, sometime. Maybe.

Could I have donated all those things we took to the dumpster that day and more in the days to follow? Could I have cut the buttons off of some of his shirts and made a memory jar like my sister-in-law did from some of my mom's clothes? Could I have made a quilt from his shirts? Could I have left his things in the closet for months or years or perhaps forever?

Yes to all of those.

But my choice was what I knew would help me get along on my path to becoming someone new.

There is no right or wrong when it comes to dealing with the everyday things of your loved one. But those things aren't your loved one's anymore. It stopped being their favorite shirt, their best-looking boots, their... whatever the day they died. Now? It is all yours. Yours to do what your head, heart, and gut tell you to do.

So, do it your way.

You're the one who has to live with your decision. Don't let someone enter the space between your ears and dictate your actions. **You got this.**

Over the next days, weeks, and longer, I cleaned out his dresser too. Socks and underwear and t-shirts. Oh, *so* many t-shirts. I thought about keeping some to wear as PJ's. I didn't though. If I was going to go on without him, I needed to go on without him as my pajamas.

Then I came to his drawer where his life memories rested. A man's jewelry box holds many wonderful and strange things compared to a woman's. Of course, his class ring and a few pieces I gave him over time inhabited its depths. There were some old tie tacks which I had never seen him wear. And watches. What is it with men and watches? Jerry's father also had a goodly supply of watches. Very strange, indeed. But hey, I am sure when I zoom off to Heaven, those left to deal with my stuff will find some strange things too.

In going through Jerry's life, there were no less than nine watches in his "catch all" drawer. Even the last watch he wore up until it was just too heavy for him to wear. By then, time really hadn't meant anything to him...

I looked through more of his things, then closed the drawer and moved on. To this day, that drawer still needs to be cleaned out. I am not really sure what to do with those items. The person they all meant so much to is no longer walking among us. I think there will always be a supply, a pile, or a hidey hole full of things that those of us left behind will not know exactly what to do with.

So, we just close the drawer, the closet, the trunk, the box and—ugh, in my case, a garage, three out buildings, an office, and his shop—and tell ourselves we will deal with all that later... You know, when it warms up. That's the one I use most of all. I will visit the garage or the shop and go through those boxes, totes, and shelves full of stuff when it warms up.

Then I think, *Hey, someday I too will be gone and the person I leave all this stuff to will have the great pleasure of dealing with not only my stuff, but the stuff of the stuff I haven't dealt with!*

That makes me tooooooo giddy for my own good. Yes. It's the girl coming out in me again.

I would be remiss if I didn't mention one more place that gets the ole heave-ho cleaning action. Under the bathroom sink. If you clean out this space on a regular basis, I applaud you. Vigorously. I do not look under there unless things start falling out or I remember the face cream I bought several months ago that promised to make my face all smooth and peach colored.

After Jerry died, I found myself searching the depths under the sink for soap. Instead, I came across doggie shampoo. We hadn't had a dog for about two years. Naturally, I forgot why I was there, grabbed my kitchen garbage can—because it is the biggest one in the house—and went to work.

Out went all the aftershaves I had bought him for countless Christmases. Medicated powders and creams for particular ailments. Shampoos that were too harsh for my tender girly head. The bottles of rubbing alcohol mixed with crushed aspirin to make those wonderful cold packs for his back, a trick suggested to us by a doctor. Rubbing compounds we used to relieve his back pain. Combs and brushes he used over the years. Old razors, blades, and cords to old electric shavers we no longer had. The list goes on and on, but I think you get the idea.

The point is, the blender in your brain is going to get a work out for sure. You'll whir calmly with the mix of your day, then hear *your* song or smell his aftershave—*Bam!* Your brain goes from chop to full-speed frappe!

> Go with the flow. Let it happen. Then pick yourself up and go on. **Memories are a gift you are left holding. Hold them, enjoy them. And then move on.**
>
> Your new you will be amazing. Move on. Always move on to meet the new you.

Under that bathroom sink was another life, one no longer here. In the following months and years, I came across other places where Jerry had piled things either needed to survive his existence or to live a life well lived.

About a year into my widowhood, I found the last anniversary card he had bought but not given to me. Because— you know—he died. He had it hidden between a stack of stencils and a box of drawing instruments he used when designing a new trailer or airplane autopilot system. That silly but loving card now sits happily on display for me on the work bench in his workroom.

Each time, each and every stinking time, something is thrown in my path that was part of him, I am surprised at the feelings I have. Some are funny, some are sad or happy, and some are maddening. Most of them still make me cry. And sometimes I get sad and afraid that one day I will *not* cry at the memories—that one day he will be all the way gone.

I have talked to people who have been a widow or widower much longer than I have been. Some under ten years and some over twenty. They all tell me that he will never be all the way gone. I take warmth from that. But! I will not get stuck. Nope, I am moving on.

I have tons—tons, I say—of life to live. I just keep moving forward.

You too. **Keep moving forward.**

9

That Warm Little Feeling

My grandmother had Brownies. Not the kind that come out of the oven and smell all warm and gooey. Although I think she could bake up some yummy brownies. No, her Brownies were these little creatures only she could see. They would sit on her bed posts and tell her the future. She had ladies who would come to her to learn of things in their lives. Kind of cool actually.

I like to think I inherited some of her soothsaying. I know what you are thinking. Yes, I do, because I can feel you thinking it!

Either you believe in some sort of spook show or you don't. Honestly, I am not sure where I sit on the matter.

I believe in a woman's intuition—and I believe in Heaven. When I talk about Heaven, I like to tell people, "Man, it must be amazing. It has to be all we think it is and more because nobody ever comes back from there." But! Yes, a Heavenly "but." I want to believe Grandma Russell (my maiden name) could tell the future and that part of her gift was passed to me. I want to believe I have a thread, a golden thread that connects me with stuff I cannot explain. There are still so many stories I have heard that tell me maybe, just maybe, before those we love go to Heaven forever, they somehow say good-bye. And with my grandma's gift, I felt it, felt Jerry bid farewell one last time.

It went something like this.

I live in a farming community with wonderful alfalfa and grain fields and cows and sheep and buffalo for as far as you can see and smell in the summer. It was probably in April a little over three months after he died (oh, those words!) when I noticed an eagle flying above my car. I love seeing those wonderful birds.

There are always some in the area. I knew a man who could look at a bird overhead and tell what kind of raptor it was just by the silhouette. I was amazed at that and so I asked him how he knew. He says to me, "Just look at the wings. An eagle has wings big enough to hold hope under them." Well, it took me a little time, but I noticed that yes, the eagle does have big enough wings to hold hope under them. So, when I saw a bird flying out in front of my car, I knew right off it was an eagle. A Golden Eagle.

Now here comes the weird part. I don't drive my car every day. I don't have to go somewhere every day. Sometime later, I was in my car going down the road to town and I noticed an eagle. Again, flying out in front of my car. Very high. Just cruising along. Wings outstretched, holding hope under them.

Okay. No big deal, right?

Well, about a week later, I was going over to a neighbor's and the silly eagle was up there again. I start to get that "warm, little feeling." I think by this time the thought that it had some meaning had creeped into my head. Creeped as in creepy. I told a woman I knew, and she patted my hand and looked at me with that "Oh, poor Trina, the new widow" look.

You'll get that look too.

And you will not like it. That "poor, poor thing" look.

Don't despair. Don't let yourself fall into and become that huddled up person whom everyone feels so sorry for. Or worse, you'll see it in their eyes. That "I'm sorry for you but really glad it's not me" look.

Shake it off! Smile big and maybe let go with a good, old belly laugh. You are going through one of life's most difficult trials. It will not define you. **You will heal.** Allow yourself to heal. Define yourself in your healing. Define yourself as the person you want to be. **Though your circumstances have changed, you are still you.**

After our conversation, I saw my eagle again. It flew in front of me so I saw it just at the top of my windshield. It soon became a game. I started to talk to it. I told it, "Glad to see you again."

I know, I know. You still think I am nuts-o. I too thought maybe I was losing it. But it gave me comfort to know those wings held hope under them. That was the hope I needed.

Pretty soon it occurred to me that maybe it was, in some strange way, a messenger from the Great Beyond. Cue the ethereal music. Order up the Brownies. Oh my stars, Trina Lynn.

Yes, I had the thought, *Hey, maybe its Jerry's spirit.* Crazy, right? It never flew along with me except in the valley where I live. It wasn't there when I traveled for groceries 120 miles away. It wasn't there when I went to my neurologist 242 miles away. It didn't even go into town with me, all of ten miles away, when I went to get the mail. It was just in the valley near home. So, of course, I started to think it was either Him or Jerry. I opted for it to be Jerry. Made me warm and fuzzy inside to think that.

Then on a bright, warm afternoon with not a cloud in the sky, I spotted my eagle as I was coming home from town. He joined me and flew out front of the car about five miles from home. As I drew closer to home, he seemed to soar higher and higher. He got farther ahead until he was about in the middle of the windshield.

At the S-curve a mile from our five-acre homestead, I saw him turn away. As I completed the second turn, the eagle continued east toward Diamond Mountain. I slowed to watch before pulling over to follow his freewheeling.

All of a sudden, the eagle caught an invisible updraft of warm air and went soaring into the heavens. He looked so happy. So free. He took off for the mountain, flying ever higher, those huge wings grabbing hope with each powerful stroke.

I knew then and there, in my heart of hearts, Jerry was saying good-bye. Going to Heaven. I took it as a sign. I watched the eagle until it was just a speck against the back drop of Diamond Mountain.

Oh yes. I cried. But those were happy tears.

Were those few memorable days with that eagle just what I wanted it all to be? Was it, in reality, what I think it was? Or perhaps it was nothing at all? Maybe it was just a coincidence and me grasping at straws? Probably a titch of all of them.

When I think of it, I know now that the warm, little feeling I felt was true. It can come in the form of you hearing your loved one beckoning you outside just as a meteorite zooms across the sky. It can be as real as a breeze through a window as your loved one breathes his last breath and blows a kiss across your cheek. It can be as real as feeling fingers running through your hair as you brush it after a shower.

One thing is for sure. I don't know if anything like those feelings can be, or will ever be, true. Nobody here on Earth does either. Not even my grandmother would have known if those warm, little feelings were true or wishful thinking. We just have to wait until it is our turn to leave and go to whatever place we believe is waiting for us. But! Until it's my turn, or your turn, to take that last journey, we can pull ourselves up and live life to the fullest. I put on my big ole wings and fill the underside of them with hope every day. Every stinkin' day.

So, test your wings. **Fly free and fly happy.** If not today, tomorrow. But fly into your new life with courage and hope.

10

Well, What About Those Rings?

If two couples lived side by side in two houses that are identical down to the red maple tree planted out front and both have back doors that squeak when they are opened, which could be 47 times a day, and both women became widows within a short time, both would be on completely different paths. The loss would be real for both, but after loss, everyone has a different set of circumstances to handle. To deal with. To face up to.

My circumstances, when the fog started to clear, had so many aspects that, to this day, I look back and still can't believe. Now, I can say that I did do some really stupid things in that first year. Said some things I should have kept to myself. Should have known better about some things. They are not really regrets. Regrets are not worth the time you spend, well, regretting them. Nonetheless, I will share some to assure you that I did them. Oh, you will have your own set of things you will do: right, wrong, and somewhere in between.

Luckily, when my mouth opened and some very unflattering but true things came out, it was only heard by a few close friends and family members during those first weeks. Looking back, I don't know what made me let loose with some of that bitterness. It was probably a mix of anger and sadness and frustration.

I was angry at him. And Him. And me. Me especially. Even though I had spent 42-plus years doing all I could and the last 20-plus helping Jerry live as full of a life as he could under awful circumstances, I was angry I hadn't done enough to keep him alive at the end. I was so mad at myself for failing him and me. Of course, there was sadness too. Unimaginable sadness. I have to tell you—even though I was sad to the point of not even wanting to get out from under the covers some days, I was unfathomably happy for Jerry to be in Heaven. For him to be out of pain.

At the same time, I wanted those closest to me to quit telling me how wonderful my husband was. I knew he was wonderful. I knew how lucky I was to have had such a good man who loved me with all that was in him. I knew he had put me on a pedestal. But I wanted to shout from the mountain tops that I had helped build that pedestal with courage, hard work, and sacrifice.

I heard from many people who, over our years of wedded bliss, had watched us and wanted to know what we had that kept us so happy. We. *We*. We were the couple people looked up to in our little community; I had heard that from many friends.

It was heady at first. Headiness, like a beer buzz or chocolate ice cream happy face, doesn't last forever. And hearing that again at such a tragic time of my life aggravated me. To my ears, it was validation that I could not survive without him. And that made me so mad I could spit fire.

At the time, I viewed my marriage—because I was so full of anger and sorrow—as an amazing thing because he had gotten everything he had ever wanted while I had sat in the background and gave and gave and gave. I knew this was not an accurate representation of our marriage and that I spoke from heartbreak, so I did my best to counter that way of thinking. I let go of such revelations that really had no place in being said. I know now it was just anger.

"Can't go back" became something I said over and over to remind myself to think, think, think before opening my big mouth to spout ugly words. Even so, letting those close to me know that my husband was a great man, but still a man, helped me in some perverse way. He had faults and so did I. We struggled in a lot of areas and with a lot of issues. But! I felt lost when someone would say that he had taken such good care of me, of us.

Well, I did too.

That stung. Over time, my anger dissolved and was replaced with indifference, apathy. Honestly, that's what I concentrate on now. We both had issues that, had he outlived me, I think he would have spouted about to his closest friends. That, I suppose, is really what made our union so terrific for those 42 years, 10 months, and 1 day. We were the same but just enough different to both pick at the stickers that prickled and enjoy the softness of marriage. Together. In private.

Now when I find myself falling into a pit of pettiness or saying something that has no value in a decision or conversation, I hold up my hand and wave it back and forth and quickly say, "Doesn't matter. Doesn't matter. Doesn't matter." The words that might have come out of my mouth just vanish and—really?—it just doesn't matter. I find that relieving. I wish I would have done that from the beginning. But I can't go back and alter what I said or how I felt. See?

Don't look back.

You're not going that way!

Before *you* read the following, please know that I am not a Bible thumper. Oh yes, I am a Christian and God is my Lord and Savior. However, I am not going to bop you over the head with religious dogma or verses. I am not proficient enough to deeply discuss the Bible. I want you to find your own Truth, whatever it may be.

That being said, when I married Jerry, he gifted me The Living Bible imbued with my new married name on the front in golden letters. Trina Lynn Machacek.

The Living Bible is written in words that are more user friendly to someone like me. You know, no thee or thou, and more he, she, and we. Inside were a few lines I keep close to my heart. Actually, I adopted these words as a kind of mantra. Remember, my Living Bible does not read like the King James Version. I think God knew I would understand His words better in the version Jerry gave me.

Psalms 141:3 reads: "Help me, Lord, to keep my mouth shut and my lips sealed."

I try to follow that and yes, I still occasionally trip on my own tongue as it thrashes about in my mouth. Sometimes I just stop

59

mid-sentence as I remember to shut the heck up! But! Yep. I know, don't go back, Trina. You're not going that way. Cool, huh?

It wasn't years for me. It took only a handful of months into my widowhood to decide to take off my wedding rings. Today, it is harder to think of than it was then.

Jerry left in January. That subsequent March, I was in Reno at a doctor's appointment with my neurologist who helps keep my Multiple Sclerosis in check. While in the city, I took my rings to a jeweler who long ago had made the third ring on my set. Jerry had had it custom made for me on our fifth wedding anniversary. I wore my stacked wedding rings and an extra smaller fifteenth anniversary ring on my left hand. On my right, I wore a wonderful three-diamond ring which boasts a one-carat diamond solitaire and two half-carat diamonds set in a platinum setting which he had made for me for our 25th wedding anniversary. See? I knew he kinda liked me.

Well, I thought it proper for my wedding rings to go to my right hand and my anniversary ring to transfer to my left. It was then I discovered my fingers on my left hand are not the same size as the ones on my right. Weird, huh? I thought so too. So I asked for the wedding rings to be made a half-size bigger and the three-stone ring a half-size smaller.

By the time the jeweler sent them to me a few weeks later, I had grown accustomed to not wearing any of them. This was one of those turning points for me. When I took them out of the box when they arrived, I knew then that I was no longer married. My marriage was over. I wasn't Mrs. Anybody anymore. I was me, standing alone against whatever was coming down the road of life at me.

Oh, I put them all on. Come on. I *am* a girl. I like sparkly things. Especially diamonds. I used to joke with people who would comment on my rings over the years by saying that I worked for and earned every sparkle. These rings are really the only jewelry, besides a watch and a cross on a chain, that I wear and a few other things that I really have.

One Christmas, Jerry surprised me with diamond earrings that were half-carat each! Wow, they were pretty. They were for pierced ears, of which mine were not. Oh, they were, long ago. I tried to pierce my ears, but it was so long between us going anywhere to wear earrings that the holes in my ears grew shut. When I got those earrings, I had my ears pierced a second time. Since we still didn't go many places to wear those sparkly goodies, the holes in my ears grew closed again. I gave up. I think that might have had something to do with him getting that three-diamond ring made for me. It drove him crazy that those diamond earrings just sat in a drawer. Anyway…

When I looked at the rings on my hands, it became clear I no longer wanted to wear anything on my left hand. So, I made the decision to quit wearing rings on my left hand, wedding or otherwise. Well, almost made the decision. I checked with a few people in my circle to make sure it was okay for me to do it. See, I questioned stuff too. I was strong, but there was a bit of unstableness to my gait on this new walk I was on. It was so soon. Was it too soon to take off my wedding rings? I see women who have been alone for years, and they still wear theirs. I didn't know what the "norm" was or even if there were rules about this big decision. It had nothing to do with any new guy in my life then or even now. No, it was about my marriage then and now.

The responses I got from my loving family and friends were unanimously "It's up to you." But it was the young man who had once lived on our property and moved to Virginia who helped me through this hard decision. The little squirt!

He said to me that I had completed my journey with Jerry. I had also completed my vows and the promise I had made with my God upon wedding. So, it was okay to take them off. He couldn't have been much over 30 years old; his words were words of someone much older. But still—the little squirt. I had kept my promise to my husband and my God, and it was time for me to move along this new life path He had put in front of me.

In saying all that, it was still another one of the big things that caused yet another break in my life from being married and a half of a twosome to being single and a one-some. HAHA. Is that even a word, onesome? Do not let that onesome become a *lone*some! Just because you are now a onesome, you have it within yourself to not be lonesome.

Remember, that lonesomeness will come and smack you in the face when you least expect it. It'll make you question every move, every thought. There is no cure for loneliness. But there is something you can try to ease it.

This is where I'm supposed to encourage you to exercise, go on nature walks, meditate, take a hot shower, call a friend, or watch a movie... You'll hear tons of ideas from friends and family. My advice? Grab a lemon slice, wedge it into your mouth, and sit there. Train yourself to equate loneliness with something you really don't like to eat. It seemed the more I did to fend off loneliness, the more I started to hate the things I did when I was lonely—something I didn't want to happen to my favorite pastime. Writing. Imagine that.

Sewing, gardening, walking—whatever it is that makes you happy. Don't do those things when you're going through a lonely jag.

I took my wedding rings and that extra anniversary ring I had sized for my right hand and put them in a little antique glass jar on my dresser that I filled with lavender blossoms. I took the three stone ring and put it on my right hand. AARRGGHH... I had it made half a size smaller so I really had to squish it on. But that is where it sits. I love the sparkle when it winks at me as I brush my teeth or as I work out in the yard and the sun hits it just right. Yep, I am a girl through and through. I like diamonds. But I have enough. Said no woman. *Ever!* Come on, I think all women have a little bit of that Zsa Zsa Gabor gene.

In the end, each decision you make will come with questions. Some will be big, time-consuming, or identity-shaking while others will be minuscule. Please don't be embarrassed or scared to ask for help. Shoot! E-mail me and ask me anything. I bet a nickel I've already thought about whatever you can come up with. Just know that this is your party; you are in charge of everything from soup to nuts. FYI my email is itybytrina@yahoo.com if you ever want to chitty chat. Really!

If you are like most people, you may get embarrassed by what can be perceived as you always saying, "Me, me, me," or "I, I, I." That will lessen. Keep in mind that in all those first big or little decisions and tasks, it really *is* all about you, you, you. I never liked the limelight put anywhere near me. I am—well, I was—a true wallflower. I felt safe and snug as a bug in a rug being just the dishwasher hiding in the kitchen rather than the life of the party.

I'm telling you without reservation, you will come out of the kitchen and sooner or later become a major part of the party of your life. There is an invitation with your name on it. Your party is just getting started. **Your party is waiting for you to**

Oh yeah—when I screwed the lid on that glass jar carrying my rings nestled among lavender blossoms, I cried tears for what had been, what was, and what was yet to come.

11

Tests, Always More Tests

After Jerry and I found ourselves without a store, farm, or machine shop to run, we fell quite unsteadily face-first into, "Well, what now?" We were not ready to be retired; we were also not in any shape physically, mentally, or financially to start another business venture. He was getting sicker. More was falling on me. Home, business such as it was, his care and life in general—it all fell into my lap. I never gave it a thought as to how much I was taking on daily. It was just my life unfolding in bites that were getting bigger and more—more life altering. Our little five acres in his thoughts were becoming unfeasible. So, Jerry started to look at moving to Southern Idaho, where he and his family and friends were from. I went along, as had become my norm. Follow his lead.

Then, he died.

In my head, I was still on that Southern Idaho pathway. The idea of me staying here, in my home state of Nevada—a state where I was born and lived all my life, the state I love and enjoyed—just never occurred to me. I was *that* married even after he was gone. I was *that* bound to what was supposed to have become of me, of us.

Winter became spring. Although Jerry had passed, our house remained on the market. I began to look at the area around Twin Falls, Idaho. A wonderful place for sure. I knew a few people there; really, the thought of living a city life was actually kind of attractive to me. Even met with a realtor and looked at some homes there. Then…

Work hard to keep track because the next few things happened fast. I should have stopped everything. But in my quest to keep my grief at bay, I churned full-speed ahead.

First, I noticed a gurgling in the back bathroom when I flushed the toilet. Thought it was just a tiny clog, so I used a plunger. Again and again. Ran a load of wash, and used water in the sewer line backed up into the shower. Not a pretty sight. As citizens of a farming community, we had our own well and septic system. I knew just where everything underground was because I was part of the twosome who had built it from scratch! From water in to water out, I knew my five acres intimately. I had helped drill the well and dig and install five-foot-deep water lines. We had done everything.

When I figured the clog needed more attention than just the plunger, I went out to the septic tank, unscrewed the lid, and got to work. A bit over a year before, we had had this same problem, so Jerry and I had built an attachment to easily snake from the tank to the house. I found the "Jerry-rigged" attachment and the half-inch 200-foot cable and began the job of unclogging my sewer. As I wrangled the cable into the sewer line, I was pleased. I could do this. It was weird to do it alone though. I was so used to having my Mr. Scooter Man at my side. Giving directions. Then, of course, me doing it my own way. That was how we worked together. No more together was going to happen though, was it? And yes, that really ticked me off.

Out there with my leather gloves on, I was talking aloud to Jerry up in Heaven with every shove of that cable. Angrily, I thrust a few feet of cable at a time. With each heave, it went farther and farther into the sewer pipe. Soon, I hit something. I jammed and shoved and finally out came... Well, you can imagine what came out of the clogged sewer line. It was at least a week since all things had flowed freely, so it was quite a whoosh and a very smelly display.

But! I did it. I. Did. It.

Then, to make sure the clog was out, I flushed toilets, filled the bath tub and drained it, and ran water into all the sinks until clear water was flowing into the septic tank. All systems were a go.

For... about three days.

The gurgling started again. Actually, I think the shower backed up first. My thought process told me to run. Run as far

65

and as fast as I could from this life. This was too hard. I was not a man. I was a woman, just a woman. I began to hate being me. I could have just gone running and screaming into the night. So very easily.

How could I find myself in this situation? Alone. Sewer backing up again in just a few short days. Mostly, the alone part tore me up. Each morning, I woke up and the heaviness of the day dawning was overwhelming. And that damned dammed-up sewer needed to be dealt with. Again.

Back out to the septic tank. Lid off. Tears of sadness and frustration ran down my face as I set up the now well-used Jerry doohickey into the stinky sewer. I shoved that cable back into the line again. At the same spot, whatever was clogging the system was hit again and—*whoosh!*—three more days of sewage came rushing out. This time, I threaded as many hoses as I could find and put them up the line, turned on the water full blast and washed out whatever I imagined was the problem.

After everything was done and the afternoon sun began to settle low in the west, for the first time, I gave thought to wanting my life to stop. Just stop. It was a fast and fleeting thought. But the thought was there. Just wanting my life to stop. I shoved that dark thought away like I was shoving the cable to clear out a line. A line I did not want to meet or cross.

A week or so later as I was sitting in my backyard, I took a good look at where I was and half-decided that this was not worth the trouble. There was too much to do, too much to handle, too much everything.

Jerry and I had toyed with moving to Twin Falls, Idaho to be closer to services he needed. We had listed our property with a realtor we knew. There was a sign around somewhere that had fallen over, so first, I went out and pounded it back into the ground so all who drove by would know I was serious about selling and moving away. Second. That next day, I went to Twin Falls, Idaho to look at moving away and moving on. I longed to be elsewhere, that way, when the sewer backed up, someone from the city had to fix it! I just wanted to be taken care of again.

The realtor in Twin Falls was nice and friendly, and I got the feeling I was not the first widow he had dealt with. He showed me a collection of homes. Funny though, as I stood on the nice new sidewalk of a nice new neighborhood of nice new homes, my mind took me elsewhere...

For the past 40-plus years, I had lived on a farm where we were the only ones around. My nearest neighbor was a mile away, maybe more. I had a gorgeous view out any of the windows of my home. When I got into a truck or tractor or popped up on a four-wheeler, I drove in any direction. Never looked around, just went. As I was standing on that new, clean white sidewalk in "the city," I peered up and down the pretty street.

Like in the movies, there were people out and about, washing cars, mowing lawns, gardening, tinkering in clean garages, laughing and living town lives. And children. Lots of children playing. They were cute and little, and the people were very nice, even going so far as to greet me and ask if I was considering moving in.

Well, weird as it sounded and as funny as it felt to me then and sounds to me now, my thoughts were, *I bet if you run over one of those little kids—they are real expensive!*

Yes. That pretty much told me I was not a city girl. So, I got back in my truck and drove home to rethink my future.

Home again, I got an offer on my property. I met the nice couple, showed them everything I was offering—the house, shop, out buildings, equipment, well, land, tools, and a graveyard of treasures. Antiques and so many cool things Jerry had collected during his tramping in the hills around Eureka before he and I met and all the cool things he and I had found and dragged home. Even the huge two-ton heavy rock we had loaded and brought home and was sitting as a decoration in a raised flower bed in my front yard, a bed and yard we created, together.

The couple saw it all and loved every aspect of "my" home and life. They left knowing my place was perfect for them. They still had to sell a business in Elko, Nevada. But they were ready to buy and move as soon as they could sell what they had and buy what I had. I watched them drive out of my yard and something, still not too sure what, inside me screamed, "Nooo!"

Not long after that day, I called my Nevada realtor and pulled my listing. She was kind and I was kind, but the couple after several emails of "I'm so sorry" from me, were not so kind. Oh, I apologized to them, but after all, and thankfully so, nothing was signed. They finally, begrudgingly, backed away.

I felt guilty for the way things turned out. In my home and shop and all I had offered, they had found their "perfect" spot. In my heart, I knew they loved these five acres and all the extra stuff I was going to sell to them. I knew that my removal of my offer to sell had hurt them. I almost just sold it to them *because* I felt so guilty, and I was ashamed to have hurt them and their dream. That would have been easy and the best for them.

But it wasn't about them, was it?

No. It was now going to be all about me.

Then, I got my head out of my rear and realized—Nobody was going to take care of me, *except* me!

This experience was the turning point. It hadn't been more than four months since he died (there are those words again). I think in all those days and nights, I hadn't stopped long enough to let myself give much thought to him never coming back, stepping in, turning up to take over, and fixing everything that went wrong. Nope, he wasn't going to pop around the corner from the kitchen to the living room on his scooter, holding his insulated cup full of Diet Coke. No longer would he put in his two cents about the sewer or selling and moving. In retrospect, realizing everything was on my shoulders was more freeing than daunting.

Finally, I was giving myself permission to make a decision, to move forward. Even if the act of moving forward was to just stay put!

That act of giving yourself permission to say, "I am in charge of me," will come. Don't force it. Let it come as it will. When it will.

And when it comes? Own it and pat yourself on the back. Let yourself be proud.

Be proud of yourself.

I had had enough with the stupid sewer problem. I couldn't flush. I couldn't do a load of wash. I cringed every time I turned on a faucet. I called around and talked to a few friends who said they could help when they had time. I knew they would do just that; friends are a true blessing. But I was not in a position to wait, so I swallowed my pride and called in a "real" company.

Sounded easy enough, right? Well, it wasn't. It wasn't easy for me to place that call. Hiring out to fix a problem was not our way. If something broke or went kaput, we fixed it ourselves. Had Jerry still been around, he would have dug up the line, found the problem, fixed it, and moved on to whatever came next in our lives. But it wasn't "we," "us," or "our" any longer, was it?

The morning I found myself using water from a water bottle so as to prevent any more liquid to go down the drain and brushing my teeth outside off the back deck was the morning that the responsibility of getting the sewer flowing fell smack dab on my slumped and worn shoulders.

It became abundantly clear that my "Trina fix" was not addressing the problem. So, a date and time was set for someone to come and send a camera up the line to see what the problem was. I was actually lucky as the company out of Elko had a couple of guys in the area who they sent over. The technicians were impressed with the work I had already done; the Jerry doohickey made it easier to get their camera into the line. Honestly, all of that made me feel pretty good about being able to—by myself—do what I had so far.

They discovered a crack which had sent a piece jutting up into the line to catch all matter of sewer stuff that came along. Subsequently, a dam had created.

When I sent up my cable, I could punch through the clog and start the ball rolling, but soon the crack would catch its prey, and the whole thing would begin again. I realized it must have been there for a long time, since before Jerry and I had made the same doohickey I was letting the very expensive sewer guys use to find the *real* problem.

The technicians said they needed to dig up the line, repair it, and recheck it; they promised to have me going again in no time. The lead man told me he would send me a proposal and estimate once they got back to Elko. No, no, *no!* "Proposal and estimate" scared the pants off me! This was going to be expensive. I was faced with spending money. Not huge money, but big money.

A few days later, I got the email. Over $2,000! Without any options, I agreed, and a few days later, the beginning of May found me standing by a hole in my lawn as two guys cut out a section of sewer line. Actually, the fix didn't tear up the lawn too bad. They used a cute little bobcat loader with the tiniest back hoe. Something this country girl always thought would be fun to run and own.

As I watched the two men work, my thoughts strayed to Jerry and I installing those sewer and water lines… at the place where we had lived together. Memories of learning to run a back hoe and a front-end loader and, of course, a shovel. Standing there, the past comprised of things "we" had accomplished slapped me in the face.

Creating a yard, plantings trees from seeds—trees that were now 20 to 40 feet tall. Pouring concrete to form a sidewalk where, for years, we had used stepping stones and boards to navigate the mud just shy of the back door. Building businesses, a home, and a life. All of that was gone, forever.

That sewer line fix not only opened up the clog in the pooper shoot from my house to the septic tank but the gates to a whole slew of life memories. A life that, after 42 years, died on January 11, 2018.

As the tears grew to the size of elephants in my eyes and began to overflow, I continued to observe the technicians. I thought how lucky their wives were. I didn't even know if these two guys had wives, but I was still jealous and mad at two women who may or may not have existed. How lucky they were as they just waited for their men to work and come home. Everything seemed so unfair.

Soon, the salty tears fell, and I escaped to the safety of my house where I stayed until I heard the tiny bobcat loader start up, signaling the hole was being filled and the fix was nearly finished. I grabbed my checkbook, pulled up my big girl pants, and went out to spend money. The first big money I had spent since being in the dead-guy place and paying around $2,700 to cremate my husband.

Money.

In my eyes, money has always been a necessary evil.

From that first gurgling in the toilet to writing the check to pay to fix the sewer line, two trips to Idaho, looking at moving to a city, seeing those children playing, selling my home, and pulling back on that sale, understandably getting reamed by two very unhappy potential buyers, realizing I loved where I lived after thinking I was supposed to move away to move on, unplugging my sewer by myself—twice—hiring a company, and watching my lawn dug up, I hadn't given myself permission to relive and remember. I hadn't realized that he wasn't coming back, ever.

All of that happened over a whirlwind of just ten days.

That was just the first test. The sewer fix was the first test. The first life-alone test I survived. A bit tattered and torn, but I survived. Then? Oh baby, then just a few short weeks later, my water well quit...

12

Testing. Testing 1, 2, 3.

From Montana to Florida, I believe everyone collects something. Just skim through the listings on E-Bay. Myself? I like little things. I have traveled a little and in my tiny life, I found it easier to stick what are commonly called "smalls" into a corner of a suitcase or backpack to bring home and look at. However, there are those who walk among us who collect bigger and usually more expensive things.

When I found myself the new widow in this Central Nevada valley, it seemed my tiny things could not hold a candle to all the collections I inherited. Not that I *didn't* own them before. But in becoming a widow, everything became mine and mine alone.

It's pretty overwhelming to wake up and find that everything that was commonly called *his* stuff, the stuff that was commonly called *my* stuff, and all the things that were *our* stuff, was now just all *mine*. Everything.

Think of that. Over and above his clothes and personal items, like the razor that had been in the shower when he passed over into Heaven, *everything* he had gathered and held near and dear over 70-plus years of living became mine. From the first hammer he had bought when he was five years old to his tools and treasures on display in our home or boxed and covered with layers of dust. All of it belonged to just me now.

I was called daily or dropped in on to be asked the same question over and over again. "Are you going to sell _____?" Fill in the blank.

I hadn't given much thought about selling much until I started to think of moving. Then it became a real thing. How would I move *everything*? There was no way on this green Earth I could move or even want to move everything I now owned. To say there were tons of things is not an exaggeration. Starting with the equipment in the machine shop that, in his last years, became his big ole personal playroom to... Well, that's where I started. That machine shop. One day. By myself. I stood out there and looked, really looked, around.

Deciding it was time, I moved forward with the next big thing on my plate—hosting an estate sale.

It was May.

The deal with a sale, be it called an estate sale, farm sale, or a yard sale, is that someone has to do a lot of work. That someone was me. Along the way, I had some great help for sure. Lifting and moving and table set up and pricing.

I was there when all the equipment we had was bought, so I knew what it was worth. But because I was smart enough to realize I was in the throes of grief, I found people I trusted—still trust today—to double check myself on the pricing. I found everyone wanted to help, but I picked and chose carefully who I let in. I knew nobody would look after me like I would look after myself.

I was lucky to have a married couple who were both retired sheriff's deputies to help with items that needed special attention at the sale. I had a wonderful young lady who, hard as it was at first for her, collected the money as things were sold. I even wrangled a great neighbor who stepped up to work with buyers to load big items with my tractor. All things considered, we worked together like the well-oiled machinery which was sold over the two-day sale.

From mid-May to the sale date in late June was a flurry of activity. Busy work kept me going. I remember sitting in the shop by myself one day, pricing as fast as I could so I wouldn't have to think about anything else. I looked up and a good friend, who had traveled cross-state to help me, came through the door. What did I do to have such a friend?

Then a couple came down from their home up by Elko, pulling their camp trailer to set up in the yard and help. How does that happen?

As the day drew closer, I had another man stop by and offer something to my soul—validation. The shop was about 20 tables full of everything you can and can't think of. It was a scary time. Was I right to move these things out? Would I be a laughing stock at the way I was working the sale? Doing it myself and not hiring a company.

Then, this man I knew came into the shop a few days prior to the sale, quietly greeted me, and started wandering through the maze. He took his time perusing the items on the tables. I kept watch as I worked. Pretty soon, he came over to me and said, "Trina, you have done a great job."

"How's everything look? Am I doing all right?" I asked.

"Your prices are right on the mark," he replied. "Not too high and not too low."

Amazingly, that is *exactly* where, in all the years of doing business in the shop, Jerry always wanted to be in regards to charging for his work. Right in the sweet spot. To Jerry, the hardest part of any job was charging a customer. He so enjoyed the work that to charge for him to do something which came so easily just seemed unfair. I tried to keep that in mind as I priced and priced and priced in preparation for the sale. To hear this friend, this Christian man who I have gone to many times since that day to double check some of my decisions with, say I did a good job meant more to me than I can ever express.

During that sale, looking around seeing Jerry everywhere was not easy. His life was laid out on plywood tables. Was I doing the right thing? Did I want to move on? Should I wait? Yes. Yes. And No.

The few times I stopped to question myself were the worst times I can remember. Of course, I could have kept it all and wallowed in memories. I found, however, that the memories were inside of me.

The day we were in Maine at a swap meet and we bought live lobsters for our employees and the stories they told us about cooking them. Those are the memories I hold dear. Not the things he bought and loved. Those were his loves; mine were more girlish.

The feelings were and still are so much more important to me than the things. On my journey, I discovered that finding new homes for stuff we had gathered and seeing smiles on faces of those who would now own them, that was what gave me happiness.

> **Find what makes you happy and follow that feeling.** Finding your happy might be just another step. It's a tough one to take, but so worth it. Just because you were the one left behind, don't let life leave you behind. Your happy is there, you just have to let it in.
>
> Knock, knock.
> Is that your happy?
> Don't just sit there. Let it in.

Just days before the sale, things continued to crop up. This was going to be the mother of all sales, the biggest of sales this area had seen in a long time. I was the first widow I could recall who was letting go of stuff. I had no children or heirs, so there was no reason, like so many families in this area, to keep everything. I plowed forward, like I was on some kind of mission.

Realizing I was going to have perhaps hundreds of people in the yard over two days, the thought of a functioning bathroom surfaced.

The most basic needs of customers over the years taught me to always look ahead. So, with the help of great people I knew in our county offices, I wrangled a company to deliver and set up a porta potty. A blue self-serve service station, if you will.

I don't know why I thought a porta potty was so important. Perhaps it was meant to enforce how absolutely insane things could get. I mean, come on. A port potty at a sale held to scatter a lifetime of collections to the wind in the middle of Nevada? How could things get any nuttier?

Oops. Spoke too soon.

Five days before the sale, the well quit.

Let me tell you what happens when the well quits. The water quits. When you say that to someone who lives in the city, they look at you like you have two heads. It's like when the power goes out on a farm, the water quits too. In town when the power goes out, the water still runs because it is usually fed to homes from a storage tank. In a rural setting, if you have a well and it quits, you are instantly without water. It doesn't take long to realize water is used for everything. This was not a good thing the week before the sale.

It was hot. I was hot. My friends who were staying in travel trailers in the yard and in the house with me were hot, sweaty, and thirsty. We needed water. I just sat in the middle of my 3,000-square foot shop and hung my head.

I was working at 150 percent capacity. I had only been into this widow stuff a short five months. There had to be a break somewhere, right?

First, the sewer.

Now, the well. I shuttered to think what else could happen.

Then?

Noooooooo. Not an MS flare up. Not now! But oh yes. Multiple Sclerosis is a sneaky little devil.

I had handled the sewer problem. Next, the well. I am truly blessed, and I know it. I called a guy, who was on my speed dial, to fix all things water.

He thought it was the control box.

It wasn't the control box.

He noticed a small leak coming from the pressure tank, so I bought and he installed the new pressure tank.

It wasn't the pressure tank.

Bless Ed, my water guru. He grabbed his crew and, in less time than it would take me to change a lightbulb in the stupid hanging fixtures I have in my living room, they pulled the pump and replaced it with a new one. Oh yes, I got to buy a band-new submersible pump too. Lucky me!

Those wonderful guys pulled up the 300-foot pipe in 40-foot sections, changed the pump, and then, without missing a beat, stuffed it all back down the hole and pressed the button on the control box. I gotta tell you that the sound a running pump makes as it pushes water up is the prettiest sound in the world when you are hot, sweaty, and on your last nerve because you are having that mother of all sales in less than a week.

Seeing water shoot out the hose hooked up at the hydrant next to the well pit, after spending a mere $2,000 more, made my heart skippity do-dah and do a happy dance. Best of all? Ed wouldn't take any pay for his work. We traded things he would have bought at the sale for his share of the bill. He was a blessing in my life for sure.

As in all parts of life, there comes a time to gather around those who not only can help but who you trust and that, if the circumstances were reversed, you would drop your life to help them too. During the years Jerry was sick, I was always building a circle around me. His doctors, therapists, lab techs, a terrific physician's assistant and his wife who, to this day, are close to my heart. Pharmacists, ambulance drivers, sheriff's office personnel in case of an emergency. EMS. EMT. All BFFs. Afterwards, I found my circle included people when I needed advice about a roof or a car or the septic or well. HAHA It's important to have a circle. It is for self-preservation.

I had a friend who was worried about calling her neighbor because she thought his wife would get all pushed out of shape. If you think that way, that guy and his wife are not good additions to your circle. Building a circle takes time and common sense. Don't overuse those in your circle but don't be afraid to call on them either.

In that same way, be ready to do whatever you need to do when you are called upon by someone whose circle you inhabit. **We are in this life wagon together.**

Don't take more than you can give and don't give more than you can afford to spare. It's a wonderful and comforting feeling to not only have a circle but to be a part of one too. **You are in charge of your circle now and forever more.**

The wagon masters of yesteryear had it right when, during overwhelming odds and strife, they hollered: "Circle your wagons!"

So, the well was handled. I shifted my attention to my stupid MS flare up. No time to deal with it. Just live through it. Multiple Sclerosis, to me, is a private battle. It is not something I talk about and really, I don't hardly acknowledge it in my life. I know it is there.

I *try* to take care of myself. I take medicine to keep it at bay. There is no cure. It is progressive. Any treatment, as my wonderful neurologist has told me, is to keep me where I am for as long as possible.

A flare up is when MS rears its head and slaps me around to make sure I am paying attention. The way it showed up during that time really wasn't all that important to this story. Suffice it to say I am a master at keeping my health to myself and that test, at that time, in the way it flared was handled to the best of my ability. It was just another test.

I remember the night before the sale lying in my bed thinking again how I just wanted my life to stop. Just stop. But there was too much to do. As time went on, I felt Jerry was leading me along a path; he wanted me to finish his life. Releasing his stuff into the world was like him letting go and letting him be freed from imaginary chains. Not holding him to Earth, but chains holding him to me.

In the days leading up to the sale as I dealt with the well and my MS, my head started to play games with me. That desire to quit was so strong.

To quit the sale.

To quit my life.

It was all so much.

As the light of the new day peeked into the bedroom window, I felt that weight lift from my shoulders. I realized that this was the way things were supposed to be.

For me to move along, even though some thought it was far too soon, I needed to let go. And to do that, I needed to see things—his things—leave. To let go of him, I had to let go of his stuff. Just like with his side of the closet. Just like the aftershave under the bathroom sink.

That short 40 days and 40 nights from May 10 to June 20 symbolized my flood. I gathered all I could carry. There were tests. Big, overwhelming tests. Not the last tests, for sure. But my first big tests. I feel like I aced them. I wasn't sure I would come out all right. Sometimes it got to be so dark in my world, I wasn't sure the sun would ever shine on me again. Shine to where I would feel like looking up and having my face warmed by those rays.

Then? That dang ole sun came back around and so did I.

In the days after the sale, I returned to the machine shop to organize the items that didn't sell. I told myself as I put items in boxes and bags and slid equipment into piles in the corner of the shop, that I would have another sale the following year. That I would not only sell the things that hadn't been bought, but all of those items I was holding back on.

Well, it has been almost three years since that mother of all sales, and those items are still precisely where I left them.

It's okay. I decided to just let some things wait until it felt right to deal with them. As urgent as it felt then to do what I did, it felt right to coast for a while. Then, it was about letting him go. Now, it's about what's right for me.

Progress.

As time goes on and I talk to more people about this widow stuff, I find myself wanting to keep moving forward. As I let go and became more open to new things, it seemed people quit treating me like I would break or break down if I were approached.

Yes, there are still days when I cry. They are getting less common, but they are still available for my viewing pleasure.

13

Different Days, Different Feelings

There was something I had to do. Of course, I was apprehensive but not afraid. I needed to go into a sit-down restaurant and have a meal. Alone. From walking in the door, getting seated, ordering, eating, and looking very cool, calm, and collected. Not a problem. HA!

This, in my opinion, was a big deal. So, as per my quiet, demure self, I jumped right in and met this challenge head on. In February, one month after my significant other's departure. I had an appointment to see my tax guy, so I popped into the car and headed out to Elko. On the way, I prepared to meet this self-induced challenge.

We had been eating via drive-thru places for a long time since it was easier than getting the scooter and all the accoutrements we were using in those last years into restaurants. I decided that I was now allowed to go into a place, sit down, and eat at a table. Like a grown-up. You know, with a fork that wasn't plastic, and I didn't have to fight a steering wheel for room to eat my meal. Not that it bothered me, mind you. I just thought if I was going to start to live a "normal" life, this might be a step in that direction.

In town, I picked a place we had visited a long time ago. I knew the food was good, and it was comfortable and home town-ish. My heart was in my throat as I pulled open the door and went in. Everything moved in slow motion. The kid who grabbed two menus asked, "How many?"

I put up one finger and squeaked, "One."

He glanced at me and then looked at the floor and shook his head like he was sad for me. I know, I know—it was just my perception.

I followed him to a *huge* semi-circle booth where I was swallowed by red squeaky plastic. I had carried in with me a file folder of non-essential papers so as to appear like I was having a "working" lunch. See, thinking about appearances all the time. I needed to stop that.

"Oh, just get over yourself" is something I used to say to myself in these types of situations. Nobody but you can know how nervous you may feel. Nobody but you can know your desire to go running into the bathroom and never come out. In a room of 20 people, there will be 20 different stories and 20 different reasons for the people around you to be there. Come on, when was the last time you were in a restaurant, store, or church and looked around and dissected why each person was there? Oh, and if you really *have* done that? *Stop!* Eating alone is not ideal in any sense of the word, but life has a way of making fun of your circumstances.

The waitress came over carrying two sets of silverware and put them down. "Do you want to order or wait for the others in your party?"

I told her I was alone and again, I *perceived* that sad look. She grabbed the second set of silverware and took my order. I dutifully scrutinized the papers in my file folder as I waited for my lunch, all the while aware of my surroundings and my aloneness. People were all around me in groups of two and four and a few families with giddy children. Everyone was having a good time, and I was alone.

Soon, a plate of fish and chips and a glass of iced tea were deposited in front of me. Now, I have to admit I was nervous during this entire ordeal. It was like being on display. Like I had a big red, yellow, and brown neon light above my head flashing, "Poor ole widow alone! Poor ole widow alone." But of course, it was just in my own mind.

As I chewed and swallowed with dry effort, I noticed the people around me were actually happy and smiling at each other.

Fresh flowers adorned each table, even the one where I sat. It was nice to see such happy couples. Then, as I sat there forcing down bites of deep-fried cod and some soggy coleslaw, it hit me. The one day I chose to make my stand to eat alone? The one day of the year that my aloneness was met head on? Yep! Valentine's Day. Aarrgghh.

I'm here to tell you that if you ever think it can't get any weirder for your circumstances, think of me, sitting alone in that big ole, red booth in a restaurant full of happy in-love couples and families on Valentine's Day. Nope, you just can't make this stuff up.

Yes, that will give you something to giggle about. I did, actually. Giggle, I mean. You can't change your circumstances; you can't wiggle your nose and just disappear. I still find it funny today that, as I sat there and really looked around, I was comforted by the fact that there was still life—full, joyful life—being lived. All around me. I took it as a sign that my life was still there within me just scratching at the door to be let out and lived.

A few short weeks later came what I thought would be a very hard day. Our wedding anniversary, April 10. We humans put a lot of emphasis on special days. As a woman, I tend to think we put an extra scoop of emphasis on such days or events. Not shooing away a man's feelings at all here. I have learned that men are just as sentimental, but in a different maybe more stoic way. We girls tend to wear our hearts on our sleeves. Men can somehow compartmentalize easier.

Then there's me. Well, of course, I am special! I am Trina, after all. HAHA!

Hiding my emotions is my forte. I can keep my curtains drawn and go about my day, insisting that nothing is wrong. During that year of firsts, I discovered comfort in being left alone. Oh, there were a lot of those days. Alone on my birthday, alone on his birthday. Who would be there to joke with me about getting yet another candle on my cake? For that matter, what cake? Our anniversary was no longer an anniversary, was it? It burned my rear to no end when my brother and sister-in-law who were married in February the year after I was married, finally passed me in the number of years they were together. I seethed inside knowing that they were celebrating 43 years. Their anniversary that year was hard for me to swallow. But it was what it was.

That first year, many days smacked me in the face. After I lived through the Valentine's Day adventure, I made a conscious effort to be more aware of the calendar. After our April wedding anniversary, along came his birthday on May 10.

I was ready.

I woke up that morning and said aloud, "Happy Birthday, Jerry."

That sucked big time.

The rest of the day I busied myself trying not to think about all the banana cream pies and chocolate cakes with chocolate frosting I had made for him over the years. I tried not to think that everyone would probably call or stop by because it was his birthday. I didn't want that—or did I? Really, how could they not know it was a special day and not stop by and commiserate with me?

Well, not one person stopped by.

Nobody knew it was his birthday. Why should they? No family to stop by. No really close friends that would know or if there were, no remembrance was evident.

I mean, really, I can't say that I know most of my friends' birthdays. And if I do, would I really come over unannounced?

When you are the one left alone, everything seems bigger and more important. But it really isn't. It is just the same as when you were a two. For the most part, days like anniversaries and birthdays were only important and celebrated by the two of us when he was alive. Why should it be different now that Jerry was dead and gone? In the end, his first birthday was a long day; the night was filled with sadness and those dang tears.

But the next day? The May sun came back up and I patted myself on the back because now I had made it through Valentine's Day, our anniversary, and his birthday.

Time moved along, and holidays like Memorial Day, my birthday in June, the Fourth of July, and on and on came and went. Each one hit me like a brick. It's not like we really did much to celebrate those times. Over the years, we had become more home bound, so the holidays came and went like snow in the summer. It hit with shock and disbelief and then melted away just as fast. Then it was time for the *big* holidays.

You know how in stores the end-of-the-year holidays start to show up in August? That is unfair to those of us who dread all that is attached to such days and weeks. There really is no fix or cure for the phenomena that will befall you when the holidays lurk in your vision. Remembering is a wonderful thing though. Remembering that now you can have any holiday anyway you want. Yes, I know, I know. I am the forever optimist. I have taught myself to try to keep on the happy side of life. Of course, it is hard, but if you have ever been around someone who loves to wallow in self-pity, you will strive with everything in you to not be a wallowing widow.

Halloween and all the kids and candy. That was the best way for me to start the marathon. I threw myself into candy. I ate so much sugar that I thought I would never stop bouncing off the walls. There are those who say sugar has no effect on your energy level. I am here to tell you that a sack of marshmallow Peeps which look like orange pumpkins and blue ghosts, followed by a package of Reese's peanut butter candy shaped to look like ghosts will definitely put some putt-putt in your butt-butt. I bought maybe 50 bucks worth of candy in one trip. And where I live, I *never* get any trick-or-treaters. So, it was all for me.

About halfway through the third handful of Halloween Gummy Worms, I thankfully woke up. My good gravy, Marie. If I could go all year and not put my head in a vat of sugar during birthdays, anniversaries, and barbecue season, why was I putting my body into a sugar coma now? Well, of course, it was dreading the upcoming Thanksgiving and Christmas holidays.

Nothing was in place to protect me from the inner struggle of those last months of the first year. I am a good cook. I do not apologize for being a good cook and loving to cook. Thanksgiving was always something I looked forward to. We got up early to put the turkey in the oven, but the big thing was to make huge amounts of stuffing and freeze enough to get us to the next Thanksgiving!

So, that first Thanksgiving was hard. But you know what? As I sit here some three Thanksgivings under my belt since his death, I don't remember what I did for that first one. I know there is still stuffing in little baggies in my freezer from the year before Jerry died. I should throw them away, but I still pull one out occasionally and heat it up—and it is just as good as the day we made it.

I am Christian, and I love Christmas and all the wonderment of His birth and what that means for me and you. However, I truly believe in Santa Clause and the magic of everything Christmas. I love Christmas. It was a struggle to decide to even put up a tree that first year. But I did it! There were even presents under it from a few wonderful friends. But I spent it alone. I still do.

In all my married years, I missed all but one Christmas with my family because it was understood that we would spend Christmas with his family. I have to tell you that I grew to hate not being able to spend Christmas in my own home. I was not asked what I wanted; I was told we were going to his mother's for Christmas Eve. Even after his father passed away, we went to her house. Even when she was moved into a nursing home, we went to be with his mother on Christmas.

So, when I found myself alone at Christmas, it was actually wonderful to spend it any way I wanted. Even today, I love—yes, still love—to spend it in my jammies and maybe barbecue a steak and have what I want, when I want, or not have anything at all. I guess freedom is pretty heady stuff.

Admittedly, my Christmastime is not something I am ready to share with anyone but myself. You just have to decide what you want, what you really want. Own it.

Then, New Year's Eve came. Now, this is the *one* I still have trouble with. Even when we were a twosome, I think we all have that one holiday that will have a boo-hoo factor attached to it. Mine? New Year's Eve/Day.

86

Since I was a young girl and babysat on New Year's Eve, I had this vision in my head. As the New Year approaches, I can see and feel the old year being ripped away. I live in an area where we get television from a Satellite dish and "local" channels from Salt Lake City, which is on Mountain Time, an hour ahead of us in Nevada. We also get television from Reno and Las Vegas. So, I can see the ball drop in New York as it happens and then the New Year being rung in in Utah and again in Nevada. Three separate times.

I feel that old year come off from east to west. My giant Band-Aid starts to peel off to reveal everything new underneath. When I say it out loud, it sounds kind of science fiction-y. It's as real of a feeling to me as if I had a Band-Aid on my knee and was peeling it off after it's outlived its usefulness. The injury of what happened is repaired and taken away with the old layer. What's left is new and full of pink and hope. Similarly, when New Year's Eve pops up, I have a hard time. It's that letting go of the past. I realize on New Year's Day that he is really gone, and I have a whole year to face by myself. That still sucks. The realization hits me hardest on that day. BUT! Like all the other holidays and life events, they pass and the wonderful sun comes up the next day, and my life goes into Trina mode with hope and happy galore.

It's getting easier as time passes. Like I tell people, the realization of his death hasn't gotten easier, but as it draws farther away, it becomes easier to deal with.

Of course, there's always a bright side. I am nothing if not one to look for something good to dig out of the trash of an event.

On Thanksgiving and again on New Year's, we always watched the parades. I know it is a big thing, the Macy's Day Parade or the Rose Bowl Parade. It is not lost on me the hundreds, if not thousands, of hours people spend on all things parade. But I don't really like parades. I admit it might be because it was like an order that I had to sit through them over and over again. Saying, "Oooo, how pretty." I tried a few times to suggest we actually go to California and see one in person. Well, that never happened. So, I sat and watched all the doings each and every year I was married. Year after year. Not the football afterwards, which I would have enjoyed. Jerry wasn't a football fan.

That first year, I suddenly found myself alone, looking at the guide on the television to find the time the parade started. Then it occurred to me—I didn't have to watch it! I just laughed. I turned on music as loud as I wanted and danced in my kitchen. Because I wanted to. To this day, I have not watched one parade—and I haven't missed it at all. I listen to any music anytime and as loud as I want and watch a little football because I want to.

Do I miss him on holidays? Yes. And every day there is something that reminds me of him and us and the life I lived. Tears still flow with tons of good memories. But again, that freedom is pretty heady stuff.

Now, just to be clear, I never felt kept from life. A full Trina life. On the contrary, life as I knew it was pretty darn good. I rarely wanted for anything. Jerry was all I could want. Strong, good provider, honest as the day is long, smart, and he loved me. Life was made easier, for and by me, to meet and exceed his desires of a good wife. He wanted to watch parades; I wanted to see that happen. He wanted to visit his mom; I wanted to see that happen. My role in life was to be a wife. I married young and inexperienced in the world of lifelong relationships and love. So, whatever made that pathway smooth sailing, I wanted to see that happen. And at every turn, I was very happy to do it all. It wasn't until he was gone that I realized how much my life revolved around him and his wants and desires. That changed quickly and—I have to tell you—happily after his death. Not at first, but not long afterwards either.

My life has changed so much. After the end of that first year of firsts, I thought I was done with all the hard stuff that befalls a widow.

Silly widow.

I heard this saying a long time ago and found myself using it as I spent more time in my new widow shoes:

"If you want to hear God laugh, just tell Him your plans."

14

Cash and The Crash

Seemingly, time never moves at regular speed. I liked it when time was zooming. Days would come, and days would go. Getting to that next day with more tasks was what I kept my eye on. Awful were the days that turtled by, plodding along from one mess to the next. The times when it felt like glue was smeared to the bottoms of my feet were the toughest. Even when the zoomier days moved me forward, there was something that made me hope for normal life to return. I tried to make the normal come back by keeping busy. It was during the times when I couldn't keep busy that I ran into the loneliness of being alone.

To get my mail or to mail letters, I have to go into town. More and more, I started to *hate* that trip. Now, please know that I do not like the word *hate*. It is an ugly word. I could use the word *abhor*, but *hate* is my go-to word to, well, *abhor*. Hate has so many ugly connotations. I use it as infrequently as possible. But I really *hated* to go to town. I would fall apart so easily, and I didn't want to be seen as weak. Seen as some poor ole widow falling apart.

Nope, not me.

Nope, no way.

I would start to mentally prepare to go to town a few days before actually going. That sounds so silly, doesn't it? To some extent, I still do it today.

The "sale" was over and summer was in full swing, and I was busy. Yard, home, life was busy. I knew it was past time to go into town and get my mail. There would be bills to pay. So, over a few days of mentally getting myself together, I gathered my courage and drove the ten miles in. The trip into town was warm, and sunny and at the post office one of the women who worked there asked how I was as I slid my mail out of my box. I just teared up and said, "Not sure I am done crying yet." She had a fearful look on her face, like she had said the wrong thing and made me blubber up. It wasn't her; It was *me*. I truly felt sorry for her to be on the receiving end of my weakness. That is exactly what I did not want to happen. I actually apologized and scurried away like a vole that had been hit in the eyes with a spotlight. I couldn't get home fast enough. I drove too fast. It felt good to drive fast. Trying to outrun the sadness that covered me no matter what I did.

When I got home, I pulled my truck into the garage and hit the button to lower the garage door. I kept the truck running. And I just sat there. I was so tired. I remember thinking, *Stick a fork in me, God. I am so done.* I guess I thought that if I just sat there, I would go to sleep and all of this would be over. Yes, I had gotten to the point of just going to sleep and not dealing with anything more. Again and again. More and more. I was that tired. I was that done with it all. It would be so easy to just close my eyes and sleep.

But! *Then...*

I recalled coming home from working in the hardware store and staying in the car to finish a song that had come on the radio. Jerry was coming to the house from the shop and so poked his head into the garage and yelled, "You're gonna kill yourself!" Man, he was mad. I was only there for the length of half a song, for goodness' sake!

What could happen? I remember thinking, *Get real!* It made me mad that he thought I was that stupid.

Now, there I sat in the garage, truck running, door closed and the radio on—and I was so tired. Just sat there, looking straight ahead at the wall of the garage. Staring at the dirt on the wall and the little tennis ball that keeps me from driving too far forward and hitting the wall that kept my bedroom and the garage separated.

A bedroom that I now slept in alone.

Now and forever alone.

As I sat there, I could distantly hear him holler, "You're gonna kill yourself."

Then, the silliest thoughts came to me. Throughout our married life, money had always been in short supply. I'm talking we had pot pies, rice, and ice tea to eat for weeks at a time. And that was when pot pies were four for a dollar! We had skimped by in silence as appearances were always something his family told me were *so* important. Nobody ever knew how on the edge we lived.

For years, I robbed Peter to pay Paul—and then robbed Peter's sister and brother too. Slowly, very slowly, things got better and a new truck was bought, or a new gun, or a new tool, or a new piece of equipment. Oh, there were vacations, on credit cards and paid off over long periods of time. Money. Money was something that was never in great supply. Then, he died.

With his death, came a tiny bit of life insurance and the realization that there were not going to be new trucks, guns, tools, scooters, medicines, trips to doctors, medical equipment, stuff off of E-Bay or Amazon (just because there was nothing else for him to do but buy things). I wasn't spending money except for food, monthly bills like phone, power, and my one extravagance, DISH TV. Money wasn't an issue for me for the first time in over 40 years.

So, as I sat in the garage that afternoon, hands on the wheel and gaze locked on that dirty sheetrock straight ahead, feeling so weary, I thought of money. I remember saying aloud, "Ah, come on, Trina. You can't end it now. Finally, finally there is some money." I still had money to spend. On myself!

Conventional wisdom and years of television and movie scenarios it seems would encourage you, at a time like that, to think about all the people who you loved or who loved you. Or to think about the good things in life. Or to think about being unable to get to Heaven because, if we're being honest here, God breathed life in me, and He is the only one who can take it out of me. You would hope that I would have thought about all of that.

But no, shameful as it sounds. I thought about money.

I still *hate* money. But I know I need it to survive. I know better than anyone that I am blessed with what I have at this stage of my life. I am happy that I can come and go as I please and help others as I see fit. Now, *that* makes me happier than I can ever tell you.

Money is a tool to work with. I am not my husband; I do not bow down to money. We worked hard, he probably harder than me, to attain what I now have. No IRA or 401k that some company matched because we always worked for ourselves. Just work, work, work and hope, hope, hope. It, money, like my MS, is just a thingy I deal with.

So, I turned off the truck, got out, and stepped into a world I thought I would never again step into. A world where I would never again have to bow down to money. I am, in no sense of the word, rich. I am not even really all that comfortable. I still have to watch my pennies every time I go somewhere. But I would be able to live life a lot less expensively than I had been for the past zillion years with my other half—a man who worked hard to make money but always thought buying and appearances were the way to go because his mother said so. Appearances were never a big part of my world.

That sounds so terrible, doesn't it? Like I blame him we didn't ever have enough money. Like I was glad he died so I could save some money. No. It was the reality of me living a life a little easier than it had been for all those years of shuffling as fast as I could to make $100 pay $1,000 worth of bills. I felt something give way inside of me. Like a string had been cut and a little light was getting through. A little spark of life was kindled inside me in the garage that day, and it grew.

That dark thought of just letting my life go, getting off the ride? That finally came to a head, and I bought it off with thoughts of money. I tell people around me that when He comes to get me, I want to die with red numbers in my checkbook. Something that I saw many, many times during my life and the one thing I hope I never have to see again. Only time will tell.

I do not know if that experience is something anyone, or everyone, or a few, or many people go through. I know that I am blessed to have come through it. If those thoughts *ever* creep into your soul, stop and think about why you are there.

There is a reason.
There is a life.
There is hope.

Heck, you can even reach out to me, and I will happily drag you forward. Why? Because, Sweet Pea, you and I still **have money to spend!**

It was late summer when all that happened. I needed a small break and thought I deserved a reward. So, I planned a short trip to Twin Falls, Idaho to visit a friend and, as silly as it sounds, to get my hair done. Okay, I wanted to get some highlights in my hair to make me feel good about myself. I figured I deserved some highlights in my life.

Driving in Twin Falls, Idaho was fun. The roads in Twin Falls were set up in such a way that five roads would intersect all at once at locations called, plainly enough, "the five points." I had to pay attention because there were so many cars, lights, and stop signs.

Remember that real estate agent I talked about? Well, even though I had decided to stay in Nevada, he graciously sent me a coupon for a free caramel apple. All I had to do was go to a store in Twin Falls to pick up my freebie. So, on the next-to-last day that I was in Twin Falls, I decided to do just that. Bebopping along in my Honda Mini Van, I missed one of those stop signs at the West Five Points and crashed into the prettiest black Toyota Truck. And totaled my van.

I woke up in my car with air bags everywhere. I could hear men outside saying, "Is she okay?" "Is she moving?" "Can you hear me?" I was okay; I was moving. I shook off that after-a-crash fog. All I could think of was the other guy. I found myself fighting the airbags to get out of the car. As I did, a man advised me to sit still. I couldn't. I asked, "Is anyone hurt?"

Oh, thank the good Lord nobody was hurt.

The man pointed out the truck's driver, and I went over and hugged him like nobody's business. He was uninjured, but his truck, the big, pretty Toyota—his baby that he had tricked out with chrome and goodies, the one that was only one payment new—was pretty messed up. By me and my stupidity.

As devastated as I was, I remember a few things about that hot summer afternoon. The police. The firemen. The EMT who asked me who the president was. I couldn't remember. I do remember telling him that I happily knew it wasn't Obama. They all laughed and determined I was fine, thank you very much.

I held onto the truck's driver, a kid who couldn't have been much over 25, and told him how sorry I was. Someone pointed out how cool it was that he and I weren't mad at each other or going at it. It was weird; I was so relieved he was okay and vice versa.

My van was really messed up. I don't know how I got out of it because the front end was pushed up into my lap. My poor car—the vehicle Jerry had researched and stewed over for months before announcing it was the car for us. It could carry his scooter so easily. It was the last car he rode in.

It was totaled.

Maybe it was His way to move me along my new path.

One more step away from Jerry. It all hit me so hard.

Letting go is as hard as swallowing a piece of dry bread without chocolate milk to wash it down. Letting life move me along was, and still is, very hard. I wanted so much for everything to stand still. Change came at me from every direction.

In reality, if you stop and think about life, change is always happening. It just feels like there is never anything as devastating as the changes that happen when you become a widow. I now know and understand that even before he died (oh, those words again), good and bad happened—and they always will. It's how I deal with them, that's the secret to keeping my nose above the water line of life.

Deal with it, then move forward.
Forward motion is a grand and rewarding motion.
Just try not to miss any stop signs along the way!

Of course, I got a ticket. And yes, my insurance went up, for the next three years! See? Money again. Me and money go way back. Now, with the crash and insurance and the poor kid who was just in my path at the wrong time, more stuff fell onto my plate. Grown-up stuff. Alone. As a widow. Everything that would have been taken care of by my husband was now up to me.

It just wasn't fair.

My trip. The trip that I gave to myself for making it through the garage episode. The trip was yet another disaster. I felt blessed and lucky to have not been injured or to have hurt anyone else, but! But I clearly remember thinking that night after everything, *Come on, God! Let up on me!*

As alone as I felt, I can now look back and see how *un-alone* I was. The man who was outside my car at my window who tried to tell me to sit still, he was sent to me. The EMTs who laughed with me were also sent to me. The police officer who kept telling me, "That's why we call them accidents" was sent to me. The tow truck driver who helped me gather my stuff from my car was sent to me. My friend Donna, who picked me up and took me to the airport to rent a car, was sent to me. My brother and sister-in-law, who drove up from Ely, Nevada to pick me up and take me home, were sent to me. Even the kid I hit was sent to me.

People were sent to me to touch my life. Every one of them was sent to help me realize that no matter what is thrown at me, it's all about making me learn to walk on my own two feet—then, now, and into the future.

This journey, this life, is precious and I now know that. Every day, every stinkin' day, I get up and—as corny as it sounds, as tough as it can get—I tell myself I am, no matter what else I am **Happy, Happy All The Time.**

15

Into The Wind... Or Not

Waking up and finding I am in charge of all things in my life is something I am getting used to. Not really liking it, but getting used to it. There are a few things on my plate of life that really scare me—like the thought of the power going off. That really frightens me. Not being in the dark; I have enough candles and flashlights to light up my world. No, it's keeping the heat on if it's cold. Or if it's summer and hot, keeping things cold in the refrigerator and freezer. It's what to do if the power is off long enough that I have to haul water because my well quits. Of all the things that people find frightening, that's what gets me—when the power goes off.

Making decisions also unsettles me. Was I right when I decided to buy the car I bought after my crash in Twin Falls? Purchasing a car is a big thing to me. It comes with all the grown-up stuff one can imagine. Insurance, tires, oil changes, and maintenance. Not to mention, does it look good on me? HAHA Yes, I am that kind of a girl!

When it came to purchasing vehicles, sure, I was in on the decision-making process. I was asked if we could afford it; I was in charge of making it so we could afford it. The rest was all about engine size, tire size, bells and whistles, and color. I just got the payment book. So, when I finally decided to buy a new car, I looked at that last thing, that payment book, and decided I did not want a payment book.

I truly hope I never have another payment book in my future. Not that making payments hasn't afforded me some really nice things along the way. We paid for and always had nice vehicles, and my home had, like, three stages of payment books. Each step had ten years of payments. That last book of 120 coupons took forever to use up. Now, my home is my own, and it is comforting to not have to tear out a coupon and send it to someone in some office someplace alongside a check so I could live in my home for another 30 days. So, I made the decision to get a car *only* if I could pay for it outright and own it lock, stock, and pink slip.

I wanted to travel by car and see stuff across the country, I knew that. I had the money my insurance paid me for my crashed car. I knew I needed something dependable; I also knew I wanted something that made me happy. Happy has become a desire that burns in my soul. I fan the flame of that desire daily. So, my brain started to think about a new car. I thought I needed something that was new because I look at that new-car warranty like it was golden. Then He stepped in and gave me an answer I had not expected.

I have a great friend who came to me via my other half. Jerry grew up in Southern Idaho and had some amazing friends when he was a kid. Growing up in a little town in the late fifties and sixties and being a farm kid, he was always working on machinery which, over the years and Friday night hot rod races, turned into a passion for building cars. Yes, my other half was a car guy, and I learned many things about cars from him. Luckily too, I got to know a few of his childhood car friends. More so, I got to know the wife of one of his good friends. To this day, we are buddies and talk often about life and all the goodies that come to us as widows (damned guys left us way too early).

We don't enjoy being widows, but we are learning together how to cope. We are stronger than either of us thought we were. She is a peach in my bowl of life. And we both love Kettle Korn, so that ties us together for sure.

It came to pass that she still had the car her other half had purchased in 2008—a vibrant, bright red zoomer of a Chevy HHR SS. It was just the car I wanted; the desire to have one of his cars was such that I cried when she agreed to sell it to me. She was ready to sell, and I was ready to buy. Worked out for us both. No amount of fretting and hand wringing on my part could have ever seen that deal coming along. I worry and worry and, in the end, no matter what my head worries about, I will be all right. We are all like that. We need to learn to relax and trust. Well, I do, so I imagine others do too.

Even if this car wasn't the right decision for me. Even if I wake up next week and realize this car was not the thing to buy, I will still be confident that I made a decision, a big decision. That's the thing I fear most of all. That I will not be able to make a decision and be comfortable in making any of the millions and millions of decisions that will need to be made. But! Oh, my car is perfect for me, and her name is Ruby. It was going to be Dennis the Menace, but Ruby fits me and her perfectly. Come on, I *am* a girl!

We have a long road ahead of us, Ruby and me. We are going to travel down life's highways and byways with the knowledge I made a decision by learning from a couple of car guys who always had time to teach me about cars—and life, decisions, and friendships that will last a lifetime and far, far beyond. Like me and my favorite other widow in Idaho who I love like a sister.

Decisions will drop unceremoniously onto our plates every stinking day. It is *how* we sit up to the table of life and enjoy the meal put in front of us that will determine the life we get to live. Yes, sometimes it is bound to be liver! *Yuck*.

More often than not, I find that if **I stop, breathe, relax, and think—think, think, think—answers will come** and the meal set before me will be something I love: *tacos!*

Another far more emotionally heavy decision I had to make that first year was what to do with Jerry's ashes.

We, Jerry and I, had talked and decided to be cremated, and I was all good with that. I still feel kinda creeped out about being burned to a pile of ashes, so I try not to think about it—much. Anyway, after he was cremated, I was left with this little box of him. It seemed to be an automatic decision to place the ashes in the Machacek Corral up at the cemetery above Eureka where he and I had installed that wrought-iron fence so long ago.

It's rather pretty up there. In the cedar trees where deer and rabbits and coyotes come and go, and the wind blows calmly through heavy boughs. Where when it rains, it smells like Heaven. The cemetery overlooks Diamond Valley where I live and is a wonderful restful piece of real estate.

Jerry liked to remark, "It's a piece of ground that once you lay claim to it, it is yours forever and you never have to pay taxes on it." That is true. He talked to one of the elders of the Odd Fellows, and we became the "owners" of a plot for four. His folks and us. There is a big Machacek head stone in the center and two individual ones on either side. His dad and mom on one side and us on the other, precisely planned by him and his mother. All very showy and Machacek like (can you feel my undercurrents? HAHA).

I will *not* be laid there. I will not spend my eternity with his mother. She and I were not friends. So, I have made my own plans with a great friend who knows my last wishes, and I am confident that my forever home is what I want.

I am not without thanks for Jerry's forethought. I did, after all, get to add a line to my headstone that he balked about: "Look out, Lord. Here she comes." It really is just a stone to mark that I was here on Earth once upon a time. As it turns out, I don't need to be there, neither does Jerry.

Oh.

Oh.

Oh.

One day while working on the cemetery fencing, I lay down on my plot. Put my hands lightly across my chest and asked, "Well, how do I look? Does it fit me?" Jerry did not see the humor in it. But he told the story several times, so I know he got the irony about it all being so final, that death stuff. Anyway, moving on.

After all was said and done, he was dead and I was left holding a little box of ashes—him, Jerry, all he was.

Those ashes brought forth a variety of emotions, especially as I struggled to decide on what to do with them. I had been up to the cemetery in the months after his death. Every time I went up to the grave site, I grew cold and distant. It just didn't feel right to put his ashes up there; it wasn't right. But where would the *right* place to put him forever be? I could wish from now until doomsday, but we didn't talk about this part. I wish we had, but the reality was it was now up to me to make this forever decision.

He loved to fish, but he fished in a lot of wonderful places. Not one stood out over and above any other. He loved the farm he worked so hard to build. But in the end, the farm was more of an albatross to us both as his folks had left us in a terrible position with their lifestyles, awful decisions, and business dealings. Though Jerry had put his heart and soul into that farm, his parents had killed it. That was so like them. No, placing him on the farm for all eternity was definitely out of the question.

He loved hunting in the Diamond Mountains, which were always visible from the east windows of our home. But he hadn't hunted in a long time due to his health. Oh, and the Diamonds are huge mountains. Where would I go?

The last time he had gone hunting, he had gone in search of chucker with the help of our golden retriever, Boomer. Man, Boomer was an amazing dog.

We bought Boomer on a whim at a pet store in Reno years ago. On the way home, he pooped in the car. It was a real boomer, so from that poop—and forever more—he was known as Boomer.

Boomer, it turned out, had hip dysplasia and no hip joints. But nobody ever told Boomer that. He and Jerry were companions for years and hunted and played together until Boomer's final days. When Jerry was diagnosed with spinal stenosis, we talked about how he and Boomer were so alike. Hard-headed and tough, neither let the pain they faced diminish their outlook.

When Boomer died, Jerry and I buried him under an enormous tree in our yard. Ever since Boomer was little, he had carried and slept with this pink stuffed dog boasting long, floppy ears. Naturally, we buried his little pink dog with him. Jerry went out to the hills, found a perfect slab of Nevada rock and carved into it Boomer's name and "He never lost a bird." We laid it above Boomer's resting place. He was about 12 years old when he went to Heaven. Yes, we believe our pets go to Heaven.

So, it came to me. Jerry needed to be with Boomer for all eternity. It had rained for a few days and the ground was ready, and I was ready, and I knew Jerry was ready to be laid to rest forever more.

I was alone.

Our little homestead was quiet, calm. I grabbed my favorite shovel, the one Jerry had used to irrigate the farm every morning and evening for years and years. Then, I began to dig over Boomer's grave. As I dug, I thought of all the things that made Jerry a man.

His strength. His laughter. That hardheadedness that built everything around me. His love of life and his dogs and cars and friends and of me. I was angry and sad, and I dug deeper and harder and faster.

I laughed as I dug too. He had taught me how to dig a hole. How to set the shovel on edge and get a square hole. How to set the dirt out of the hole close to the edge so it could easily fill the hole around a post that would surely go into that hole. Pouring out his ashes that day, I filled the hole with his whole life. A silly thread of ashes that was him for 73 years. The earth was moist and smelled so good. Rich and full of life. Pretty soon, I was half a shovel handle deep and something kind of rubbery stopped my progress. I put my shovel in the hole and it sort of bounced back. I could see something in the hole. It was an ear of Boomer's little pink dog. That was far enough.

I opened the plastic box that held Jerry's essence and laid his ashes in that hole that I dug with my own two hands and his favorite shovel. Placed him with his best friend with whom he had such a connection for so many years.

I know they were both there watching me. I was so at peace with that decision. I didn't scatter him to the wind. I found his forever home, and it was perfect. The perfect decision. To this day when I walk by, I can see the two of them playing with tennis balls in the yard. I can see Boomer carrying five—yes, *five*—balls in his mouth, showing off. I can see all the men who would come to the shop and play with Boomer over the years. I can see Jerry and Boomer getting ready to go bird hunting and the excitement on both their faces. Yes, that was one decision I made by myself that I treasure. It taught me that if I can decide something that huge, I can face whatever is to come.

Let the power go out. It will come back on. Let me get down and out and feel cooped up and get itchy feet. I can always just get into my little Ruby and travel down the highway of life and live the best life I can. Besides, there are still far too many tacos waiting to be eaten. Grab a napkin and enjoy your meal. I know I am going to.

16

Forward, Backward, Up, & Down

I wished that when I woke, my world would *finally*, miraculously, make sense. I wished that I would feel normal again. I wished for this "E" ticket ride to stop so I could get off; my head was spinning. I wished that when my eyes opened, for just a split second, all the ick would dissolve and give way to calm water. But the rushing hurricane with gale-force winds always blew away what small chances of peaceful waters there were, and the ick remained. Oh, there are a zillion words in the dictionary to describe those morning feelings, but "ick" covers it pretty well.

Life was pure ick.

It was time to pick some ick off. That happened about seven months into my new sightseeing tour of life.

Drinking. I had a father who drank. Not to excess, but occasionally too much. That was always with me. In my mind, I never saw him as an alcoholic. Maybe a bit of a functioning drinker but not a movie-of-the-week alcoholic. That was my thought process when I had a beer or margarita. I would tell myself, *Don't let go, Trina. Don't enjoy yourself too much or Jerry will get mad.* That kept me in check. So, when I found myself without my other half watching me, I called a good friend, who I had not been able to see much during my married life, and asked her if she wanted to meet for lunch. Happily, we made plans.

She lived in Ely, Nevada, a town some 70 miles east, so I popped over to visit. It turned out to be just what I needed to break the string holding me in the "be a good girl" aisle. That lunch turned into a 24-hour period that knocked me back into the world of the living.

My friend's name is Goosey, a nickname I crowned her with while on an adventure in the seventies. Sometimes, it's shortened to just Goose. We met for lunch, and over tacos and diet coke, I started to breathe a little easier. We met in the eighth grade and were as close as two friends could be until she married the year after we graduated high school. Her life understandably changed and moved her away from me as my life continued on the party pathway. Even though time and a few miles separated us after I got married and moved away, over that lunch, we picked up where we had left off. We were now both widows, her for some years and me for some months. Oh, how I needed to just see her.

Goose was a bartender, but it was her day off, so after lunch, it just felt right for us to spend the day doing whatever we wanted. Our first stop was to pick up some ice cream and take it to her daughter who was tending bar at the establishment where Goosey worked. We delivered the treat and had a beer there. Then, someone bought us another, and we sat and talked and drank. Soon, another beer appeared and we talked more. Laughed and carried on like those 40 years apart had never happened. But, of course, they had and we talked about them, about how we let the men in our lives actually keep us apart.

Eventually, we were off to the next watering hole to visit another friend of hers and continue our journey down memory lane. The talk was about her life and the man she had married and buried. She smokes, so I talked about her health. In her reply to my concern, she admitted to me that sometimes she wished to be reunited with her deceased husband. To her, health didn't matter; she lit another cigarette. I discovered she and I were sort of in the same place in our lives, and so we discussed the men we had ended up with and when they had died. It was well before my "garage" episode. But her words rang so clearly, it kinda scared me. Not for me, but to think that someday I could lose her. I pushed that away. To lose her after finally being reunited seemed to come out of left field and terrified me. But the day was not about being sober; it was about freedom and friendship.

Then another beer appeared like magic because we were at the bar where everyone knew her. As the afternoon wore on, the beer just kept flowing. I bought, she bought, and someone she knew bought. A beer or two later, we laughed at the fact that it took us all those years of growing up to be back where we were when we were much younger and still drinking and talking about boys.

I asked if she would ever remarry. "No!" she replied without missing a beat. Her life was happiest with the man who made her a widow. He was her second husband and truly the love of her life. Nope, she had no intention, thoughts, or desires to begin anew. That really surprised me. I don't think I thought a lot about her moving on with someone else. I just took it for granted that after some time she, and probably I, would meet someone else and start the life of a twosome again. Isn't that what is supposed to happen? Kinda like a divorcee who goes on with life with someone new?

Huh.

Guess I hadn't thought about it. Much.

Of course, I thought about it. After all, *I* wasn't dead. *I* still had life to live. Would it be alone? Forever? *Yikers.*

I remember looking at the two of us in the mirror behind the bar and thinking, *I shouldn't be here. I should be home. I should be ashamed of myself for being here. Jerry would be disgusted that I am here.* I got so mad at myself for feeling guilty, for having fun. How could I be having the exact type of fun he had spent all those years keeping me from having? Had I learned nothing from him? I was not supposed to be *that* kind of person. As per my usual, I started to think I should get my butt home. I think Goose saw that "run away" look on my face because she ordered me to have yet another beer.

Talk between Goosey and I traveled to what she had thought of Jerry and what I had thought of her first husband. We both had the same somewhat unflattering opinions of each other's choices. We were in lust when we met our husbands, her first and my only. We loved with all our hearts, and life took us on some wonderful, strange, happy, sad, and amazing adventures. We talked about her kids, one of which is my goddaughter. Yes, that is how close we were. I am the godmother to her first born, something that, to this day, I know her first husband did not agree with. Now, after all those years, we remain close. So, we had another beer.

We talked and laughed and drank, but not to get tipsy; it wasn't about the beer. To me, it was about the freedom—and the guilt—of being there. We discussed what we should do next. Well, turned out that that daughter of hers (my goddaughter) ran another bar 30 miles south of where we were, so we bid everyone a hasty farewell and headed out to see what trouble we could cause elsewhere.

We stopped to gas her car and grab some munchies, then off we went to continue our adventure. The day was turning out to be just perfect. Just what I needed. A little bit of me felt guilty, and a whole lot of me was excited to feel that freedom from everything. No responsibilities of having to be somewhere, doing something, getting something done. No one looming at home, looming over me to answer too. It was so weird; I felt a bit uncomfortable. After all, it was over 40 years of having my feet held to the fire to be just so Machacek perfect that letting go and having fun left me a little off kilter. It was a relief to finally have someone to talk to who wasn't afraid to tell me things I needed to hear. That I was going to make it on my own. That I was not the first person to lose my way and gain my footing again. That it was okay to feel mad at the world and sad for myself enough to curl up and kind of die inside. That the guilt of relief I felt when he died was real and would dissolve into memory—eventually.

Goose was more accustomed to having beer in her system than I was; I was content to let her drive as I could just sit and giggle and talk. And she just let me go on and on. It was safe and comfortable to be with her. She had my back, and I let her take care of me. How could I have ended up with such a great friend who, after all that time, was still there to catch me as I fell? I must have done something right along my life's pathway.

By the time we got to the next bar, the sun had gone down. We had another beer. Although my beer-drinking days were far gone, it just felt right to finally be able to sit and drink with

Goosey. In my married life, she was not allowed to be someone I could associate with. There was something in Jerry that kept me from my hometown, my pre-marriage friends, and, to some degree, my own family.

Jerry and I met when I was 20. I wasn't wild perse, but I was having a good time in life. Apparently though, when I said, "I do," I had tacitly agreed to "I won't do *that* anymore." Honestly, I didn't even realize it had happened until after his death and I was sitting there at the bar with a friend I had missed so much over the years. In no uncertain terms, Goosey told me things I knew I had let happen to the Trina I was long ago. More than just growing up and being married. She told me I hadn't been the same after I got married and it was time to get that girl back.

Maybe I let my Trina die inside of me a little, but I never admitted it. I was the best wife I knew how to be, and I know he loved me and we were good together—but I missed that girl I was. I told Goose that since Jerry's death, I had slowly been making my way back, older, wiser, and with some Machacek in me, but with a whole lot of Trina too. Finally, Trina was going to be allowed to live. Strange how I grew up a little more that night. It was a true awakening. Oh, and I was ready. I was so ready to live again.

Goosey was as nutty as ever, and I was as crazy as she remembered. We laughed and cried. I told her I was talking with a guy we had known when we were young, but that I wasn't looking for anything but fun. It was all on Facebook; he lived in Idaho somewhere. At first, Goosey was okay with it. Oh, but when I told her who it was, she gave me what for!

"He's not the guy for you," she asserted. "He's bad news. What are you thinking?" She told me I was naïve. That I had no idea about guys and all that came with it. She was right. Even though I had some good times in the few years between high school and getting married, Jerry was the first guy I really went out with. He was the first and only guy who came to the house to pick me up for a date. My dad really liked him. So, when Jerry asked me to marry him, of course I agreed. I had been naïve. Goosey told me as much without batting an eye. Oh, and she told me to tell the guy with whom I had reconnected to take a hike. We laughed when I countered her reprimand with, "Hey, you're not the boss of me. And neither is anyone else!"

Night descended on us. Luckily, the place out in the middle of Nowhere, Nevada where we ended up was not only a bar but a sort of oasis that had extra rooms to crash in for the night. After lunch and beer and hours of talk and beer and laughter and learning and growing up, I flopped down, my head spinning, and fell asleep. It was a grand time where my life went forward and backward and up and down. Every emotion was tested and retested, and I had come out more alive than I had been.

I woke up at about 5 a.m. Everyone was still asleep, so I went out front to the bar and sat at the window and watched cars and trucks go by on the nearly deserted highway that led to Las Vegas some 240 miles away. Sitting there wishing I had a toothbrush, it hit me that I actually could go out and have fun again. Not go crazy—like some of my friends who had gotten divorced and gone off the deep end into booze and men. I could meet with friends and enjoy myself and still be in control of my life. I had been afraid to see just how far I could throw out my rope before I hung myself. I had plenty of rope; it was going to be okay.

About an hour later, I returned to the rooms, woke my cohort, and said, "Goose, I gotta get home." She got up and asked me if I wanted a beer. HAHA No, I was up to the full mark. Then, she and I went back to Ely.

A few hours had passed, but that time was better than any I had spent in recent years. I was Trina again and I headed home, back to Eureka. Radio blasting all the way. Then...

Oh no, that isn't the end of that story. It should be, but it was really just the beginning of the next chapter of my new life.

See, that's the thing about this widow stuff. Just when you think you've gotten it all figured out and are ready to settle down and get into the groove of your new life, something new and exciting bowls you over. At first, I balked at everything that tried to change my course; I almost fell into a sad dreary rut of the same person I had been all those years of my married life. But the 24 hours I spent with Goosey taught me to just let life happen. Roll with the punches and see what comes of it all. Some things will be more ick. That is to be expected.

Then there are the times when the ick is replaced by wow—if you just let it in.

Let your widowed self be *wowed!*

When I got home around ten that morning, I began moving the water on the lawn which had been in the same place since the day prior. A few minutes later, a little, white Toyota pickup pulled into the yard, came up to the house, and parked. A young man got out and meandered over to me.

Dressed in clothes I had worn two days straight and that probably reeked of bar and beer, I just looked at him. He hesitated a few moments, gave me a sheepish smile, and then asked, "Is this place for sale?"

17

Holy Cats and Kittens, Batman!

My reaction to the question took me by surprise. The answer in fact was, "No." Nope. Not my home. Not the place I had worked so hard to develop for 40 years. Not the yard with the trees we had planted from seed. Not the lilac bushes that I had watered and grown year after year that had magically, finally bloomed that first spring after Jerry died. Not the shop where I had learned how to weld and cut metal and swept the floor for some 35 years. Not the office where I had robbed Peter to pay Paul to "keep a bean on the table," as my dad would say. Not the home where the wood stove Jerry built from a 30-gallon barrel had burned wonderful fires during gray days to keep us warm over many winters. Not my kitchen, which boasts the cutest porcelain knobs with tiny cobalt windmills on each cabinet and drawer that I had designed. No, none of it was for sale.

What in the world made me think I should, would, or ever could leave my little corner of Heaven? I was tired of running from my future. As bleak as I thought it was going to be, I knew it was up to me to make my way back into the world.

It had started that morning after being out all night and now, as I stood on my lawn that needed to be mowed and fertilized and the trees needed trimming and the flower beds needed weeding, I felt a familiar sensation. One that I've tried to explain to others over the years. It goes like this…

I am underwater. As I float there, I release some air out of my lungs to create a collection of aggregating bubbles. One big ole bubble rises lazily toward the surface, sparkling in the sun. The bubble—and the surface—are just out of reach of my hand. I swim after it to give chase, but find it's faster than me and stays at fingertips' distance. I realize I need to get to the surface for air, so I kick harder, swim faster. I can't breathe!

For years, I've felt like I was swimming up through an infinite column of imaginary water, forever trying to reach the surface. But I'm always drowning. All I want is that breath of air, that little reprieve that would let me relax, maybe pay *all* the bills that came due. Just once, in full. To breathe would mean I could complete the work piling up in front of me without more being tossed my direction. House, meals, shopping, running a business with books, employees, orders, and bills—always more bills.

If I could just breathe, I would be able to rest. At first, it was farming, a job with few rewards, especially if you subsisted at the bottom of the totem pole where, more often than not, I found myself. When Jerry's parents lost the farm to foreclosure and before we returned life to the failing establishment, there was running, cleaning, and helping in the shop. Then, the work load of the hardware store came into my life.

Work, work, work.

Life, life, life.

There was always the yard to keep up in the summer and snow and ice in the winter to deal with. Throw in his family (really, his mother and her demands).

Over the years, my responsibilities began to include tending to Jerry and his health, which included timing medicine, making appointments, meeting doctors, tending to insurance and medical bills, and—without reservations—helping Jerry live his fullest life possible. The list of things that was expected of me was endless.

Yeah, yeah, it sounds like I'm poor me-ing, doesn't it? I didn't live like that. I never stopped long enough to feel like I was being put upon. But I did always feel as though I couldn't catch my breath, as though that necessary bubble of relief was always just out of my reach.

Years of struggling to pay bills, get work done, be healthy, and be truly at peace made obtaining that breath impossible. Jerry died and the surface got farther away, and I sank into cold, dark water.

Then, that clear summer morning came. I was asked if my home was for sale. I finally knew where I was going to live, where I was supposed to be all along. Sounds easy now, in hindsight. It was, though, just that kind of bubble-popping moment. I would never have thought that making the decision to stay put would bring calm to the mess that was my life.

Oh, I still chase that bubble. I am ready to always have a bubble to chase after. But! I have finally seen something that was always there. I was just too wrapped up in feeling angry about having so much on my plate to discern what was right in front of me. I always saw the bubble rushing toward the surface above me. The bubble sparkled in sunshine, filtering through clear wonderful water with a blue sky above it all. How could I have missed that? I had looked past the water around me, thinking it was mud. It wasn't. It was clear, clean, and refreshing. It wasn't much. Life wasn't drudgery; it was pretty easy to swim through. I was a strong person, a strong woman who handled anything life threw me. How could I have not seen that all the stuff I dealt with, that I thought was choking me, was just life? And I had made it through the hardest of trials and still stood.

But! Shouldn't there be a plan? Shouldn't I have some direction to life?

There are always more questions than answers. It takes a long time to realize that just because there are questions, answers will not follow. And when they do come to you, they come in strange ways. Could be a letter from a friend. Could be a hand on your shoulder that you feel warmth from.

Nothing, of course, is a guarantee. But I am willing to bet a nickel—yes, a whole nickel—that at some point on every widow or widower's journey, even though you may never get all the way to your surface, **you will realize that the water you are swimming through is clear and refreshing and you can see your way to your surface.** It's been there the whole time. Yep, I'd bet a whole nickel.

It isn't very often I just sit and think. Might strain my brain or cause smoke to come out of my ears. Thinking, as I have heard, is a thinking man's game. I don't know too many people who just sit and think. If I sit for more than a few minutes at a time, I get bored—or fall asleep. Neither are things I want to do. Well, maybe an occasional nap.

It was exciting to realize that there's a lot of living I have yet to do. That thinking happens on the fly around me. It's been that way since I was a kid. It's too easy to get stuck in the muck and mire of life if I just sit. So, I had to force myself to sit and think about what Trina wanted. What did *I* want to make of my life? Not like I would ever stick 100 percent to any plan, but at least I figured it would be smart to think about it. Form some sort of Trina life plan. I decided I needed something to work toward.

Oh, I thought about volunteering and maybe even getting some kind of part-time job just to be part of something. Well, by now, I was pretty happy being somewhat retired. The thought of having to be some place at some time and giving up the nice afternoon naps I was growing accustomed to having… I ditched the "get a job" idea pretty quickly.

I am blessed and lucky. Through years of hard work and determination, sacrifices and investments Jerry and I made together, I have been left in an okay place money wise. I am not rich, nor do I think I ever will be. But I am comfortable in my shoes and in my checkbook. I will always need to watch my pennies, but I have been doing that for so long, it is an automatic reflex. Guess that is part of my "bubble" watch life.

114

With my thinking cap on, my pathway came into view. It was pretty easy really. I wanted to write. I love to write. When I was in school, I wrote little stories and limericks. I wrote a book-like story the summer after I graduated high school. I wrote it longhand at the kitchen table where I would regularly leave it. I was surprised to find that my mom read what I wrote every day. If I missed a day or two, she nudged me to keep going. She was my biggest cheerleader in my life. I was too wrapped up in being a teenager to see that nudging as a life path, and she didn't know how to guide me forward, so my writing just sat on the table, metaphorically speaking.

Don't Go Back, Trina. You're Not Going That Way!

Then I graduated from high school and instead of going off to college, I got a job as a telephone operator in Ely, Nevada. That was, hands down, the best job I ever had. When things got slow or I worked graveyard (I loved working graveyard), I would write little rhymes and stories on these two-by-two-inch pink notebooks we had at our stations. Nothing exceptional, just jotting and scribblings. I still have some of those stories hidden away in my cedar chest. My treasure chest of the past. I am such a girl; I keep everything that means anything to me.

Even though I graduated thirteenth in my class, I missed the college boat. I was too busy playing in life. Then I got married when I was 20, and I found myself a newlywed working on the family farm. The first year I was married, I got hold of a *Country Woman* magazine and thought I would write about being a new "city" girl on the farm. I wrote a short story and what do you know? I sold that story and got a check for $75! I was so excited. Maybe I could write *and* be a farmer's wife.

I was pretty stoked when that check came. Before I cashed it, I made a copy of it, put it in a frame, and hung it on the wall in our office. It was just a few days later when I was working in the office on a new story that the hammer came down on my writing. Jerry told me in a calm but firm voice that I was not to spend my time writing. I was a wife and any extra time I had would be used doing wife stuff. It was that clear and that final. So, my writing career ended just as suddenly as it started. I did keep that copy of the check up on the wall though. That was the spring of 1977.

Zip forward to late 2012. Jerry was spending more time at home. He couldn't get out easily to go into town to be running our hardware store due to his pain, so it fell to me to be there. I found myself needing an outlet from the work at home and at the store so, for some silly reason, I wrote a story about Christmas. Something inside of me was itching to have an outlet from what my life was turning into, and writing let me be somewhere else. A *happy* somewhere else. To this day, I still love that Christmas story.

(If you are interested in reading "The Blue Box," see the back of this book for a free copy. Really!)

In our little town, I know a lot of people and the places where they like to gather. So, on a lark, I posted my story around town on bulletin boards and on tables in break rooms, just to give those who happened upon it something to smile about. Pretty soon, I got nice words back about that story. I even let Jerry read it. He laughed and seemed to enjoy it. I like to think he knew I needed something to keep my sanity in our somewhat insane world. The pain and pain medicine along with that damned stenosis and work and everything else we were dealing with caused us both to look for ways to keep our sanity. For him, it was keeping his hands busy, be it constantly working on his scooters or anything in the shop or with guns or cars. He softened a bit about me having something else to focus on, i.e., writing. I needed some way to escape, to find something to laugh at. Making him laugh was a big plus. Finally, I was writing again.

Then, I was on a roll. I wrote a few little truisms in short-story form. When I was feeling my oats, I decided I had nothing to lose, so I called the editor of our local newspaper. I asked if he would like to run a collection of them for a few weeks. Apparently, they were all right as he agreed to let me write for the *Eureka Sentinel.* And that is how my weekly column "Is This You?" was born.

Jerry finally agreed that maybe I could take time to write. With his seal of approval, I ran to my computer, and I have been writing like a crazy woman ever since. Happily and with some pride, I can say I have never missed a deadline for my column. Even the week in January 2018 when Jerry died. He died on Thursday at 2:30 in the afternoon. I had that week's column done the next day and sent out on Sunday. It was about watching him those last days, his last laugh, seeing him finally at peace, and knowing that he zoomed to Heaven. I got such an out-pouring of love from so many readers the week that column was published. I still feel that warmth.

That is absolutely why I write. To give a smile, make life a smile for someone, somewhere.

"Is This You?" has grown since 2012 and is read weekly in papers in several states. Growing all the time, thanks to the Lord. Pretty cool, huh?

After thinking about what to do with my life now that I was the newest widow on my block—HAHA, I'm the *only* person who lives on my block—I found that all I wanted to do was write. Now! Holy cats and kittens, Batman. Excited was an understatement.

What to do first was kind of heady. I mean, you don't just—*poof!*—write and become the next Stephen King or Harper Lee. Oh, if it were only that easy! It is a business, an aspect of it I am still learning about. I got the writing part down. I think I do, anyway. I tell this to people who ask me where I went to school to learn to write. I did not go to any school, except high school. I emotionally tell people I think of my writing as a gift from God. I do not want to throw a Bible at you, but I believe that to be true.

Knowing how happy writing makes me feel, I finally realized how Jerry felt when he made something from metal or wood. To create something from nothing is the most rewarding thing. His gift was his ability to build or fix anything, and now I understand how great that magical feeling is. I think that was a big reason he never quit living, never quit building and fixing and teaching me, even when he was in pain. Being responsible for my gift is a big job. I absolutely am amazed that I can sit down and create a story from letters and words, from nothing to something. That gift is one that I am ready to realize and take on.

When I sit down to write, the words seem to fall out of my fingertips. It is the most amazing thing to feel. I could tell you I went to some la-de-da school and have tons of diplomas that show I have learned to write. In actuality, I just sit down and write. It is not lost on me that it is so amazing. It took me all this time to see that Jerry had that same push in his life, to live and create something from nothing, and his desire to make it. He told me once that when he died, he was going to ask God to line up all the things he worked on and made during his life so he could just look at it all. I hope he got to do just that.

I thank God every time I start and every time I finish a piece. So, to decide to write in my spare time, now that I have spare time? It was a no brainer. I have to admit though that I have zero smarts about selling myself. I still need to work on that side of this writing business. I will. I will get it, eventually. It's good to not know *everything* about the things you like to do. That not knowing keeps you on the edge of your seat. Learning is how I meet people and enjoy talking about what I love to do. See? This moving-on stuff is rewarding in that you get to do what you enjoy, and it gets you back out into the world. It's a big world, full of all the stuff you see on television. People, food, fun, travel, and experiences you may have dreamed of and now—you get to do it all. Sadly and happily. That's life, isn't it?

I think everyone has something inside that they can and hopefully want to do. Finding that "thing" and doing it because you have the time, that's part of becoming okay with being a widow. You can enjoy cooking, cars, sewing, wood working, music, hiking, gardening, welding, painting, feeding and watching birds, volunteering. The list is endless. The time is yours. What could be more perfect? Time and desire coming together at a time when you feel like you're at your wit's end. Oh sure, it will take time to be comfortable. After all, there were probably years where there was no time to spend on your desires. Learning more about whatever is your life's desire turns into a grand plus in your new life. It pushes you back into the world.

Now?

Now, you have to give yourself permission to spend your time on you. It's okay to do just that.

Spend *your* time on *you*...

18

Friends, Friendship, and Friendly

Let me get right to it. Being alone sucks. Not all the time but maybe 74 percent of the time. The other 26 percent is while I am sleeping or having popcorn for dinner. That is an exaggeration, of course. Except for the popcorn. But I know that my time can be spent in abject misery if I let it become abject misery. It takes work, really hard work, to fend off abject misery.

Well…

I think that is enough use of the words, abject misery.

Time and time again I have wondered what life would be like had Jerry not died. I suppose it would have just continued along the path upon which we were traveling. It hadn't turned out the way we had dreamed and talked about as we grew closer to retirement. We bought a motorhome, the one giant extravagant purchase we made with money from the sale of the "family" farm. Most of the money went to his mother. Another life decision I was not privy to, otherwise I would have spoken up loud and clear. BUT! Don't look back, Trina. You are not going that way. Hmmm. Seems to be a theme to my life… Yours too—**don't look back too much or you'll get stuck there**.

Our motor homing plans included at least one long trip around the entire country. We never got to take that trip. It was a pipe dream; I think I knew it was all along. That trip would have taken at least a year. A year that we were going to enjoy after we sold the farm and our business and had a pot full of money we could use in any manner of silliness. But life makes for squirrely endings to happy dreams. Not making excuses here, just stating what happened.

Because of medical bills and Jerry's circumstances, we found ourselves having to take about one-fourth of what we expected to get from the sale of our business. In the end, that money barely covered the costs. On top of that—and the cold, hard fact that the farm money got sucked up by other means that I will explain later—we spent most of our time in the motorhome while it was parked in various hospital parking lots before, during, and after operations and rehabs. It was an expensive motel, but it was comfortable and I could drive and park it and work all the motorhome goodies. Apparently, what I have heard more than once and said in these pages is very true. But they again need to be said: "If you want to hear God laugh, just tell Him your plans."

In losing Jerry, I gained something that surprises me still today. Friendships. Oh, I have always had friends. What I got used to calling "at arm's length" friends. Not because I wanted it like that. It was just the way it turned out with Jerry being sick and, well, just being Jerry. He liked his privacy and the solitude of living away from civilization, going so far as to express interest in painting the bathroom totally black for extra seclusion—something I did not ever allow! I wonder what he was trying to hide from. I hope it wasn't me. I like to think it was from his parents and all they put him through over the years. I will never know.

I too enjoyed the solitude to some degree. Life was easier when I finally figured out that going with the flow of *his* life was better than continuing to beat my head against a dam. I often craved friendship, even if it had to be at arm's length. Not having close friends was easier than trying to scoot around the questions of who, what, when, and why I didn't seem to have very many friends. I found it easier to act like I was shy. I suppose it helped further my case that I had low self-esteem. That fit into my persona quite nicely. Especially because my self-esteem has always been low. Hmmm. Oh, all that is such another story.

Please don't think my life was spent in a closet. No, it wasn't like that at all. Jerry was a terrific man and husband. Ours was a relationship built on trust and love and patience. Yes, I was somewhat kept under his thumb. A soft thumb, but still in no uncertain terms, a thumb.

Now? Oh now, I don't have to answer any of the questions of what my plans for the next minute, day, month, or year are.

Now? My life is mine to do with what I desire and no, that doesn't mean traveling in a motorhome. I want. Well, to be perfectly honest, I have no idea what I want. It's easier to know what I *don't* want. And I don't want to ride around in a motorhome. So, I sold it.

I printed off the following little ditty and taped it on my back door so I see it and remember to feel this way as I go out into my new world.

Today is the beginning of my life.
How I live it from now on defines who I am.

As I watched the motorhome leave my yard with the two new, excited owners in the captain seats, it was kind of like selling another part of him, his dream. It can be sad to wake up one day, a widow, alone with no direction. The day I sold the motorhome was a day I had looked forward to ever since we signed the papers to buy it and drove it home. I had known all that he planned for, all the magical travel and out-of-reach trips, would probably never happen.

Come *on*!

I was doing the books for all of our married lives and knew it was not something we would ever be able to do. The only reason we were able to buy that monster was because he sold the farm we had bought back from the Farmers Home Administration (FHA) after his parents went bankrupt. For the uninitiated, the FHA has ruled that when a family farm is foreclosed upon, the land is immediately offered to other family members. So, due to some complicated circumstances and government programs, we were able to purchase the Machacek farm, plant it to a cover crop, and—over ten years—pay for the purchase with the money we received from *another* federal program called the Conservation Reserve Program (CRP).

We paid the farm off and should have been ecstatic. It was 900 acres of beauty that Jerry put his heart, soul, and back into to build for the family. Unfortunately, the "family" ended up being just his parents. For years, Jerry and I worked toward becoming partners with his parents. In the end, however, we were just another couple of hired hands. The partnership never developed. It broke my heart to see Jerry lose that dream.

The part of the Bible that talks about honoring Thy Mother and Father was a huge point of conflict for Jerry. He was a better man than I was a woman. I got mad, but he kept honoring his mother no matter what it did to our future. Because of his mother's self-induced and self-serving needs and her "keeping up with the Jones'" way of life, we found it increasingly difficult to stay ahead of her. Jerry, it turned out, was her greatest—and truthfully—only source of income.

Jerry's mother grew up in an era where appearances mattered, regardless of cost. And it was her *costs* that caused us to sell the farm. I look back now and think of that time and feel anger swell up inside of me. The money she spent… It was a dark and ugly time for me. I wanted to scream about how she…

No, no, no. Don't go back there, Trina.

As I said, we used part of the money we earned from the sale of the farm to purchase the motorhome, but the majority of the money went to his mother. Because—as it was explained to me many times—she had ended up a poor widow. Prior to the death of her husband (Jerry's father), they had declared bankruptcy due to bad money management. Jerry had taken care of her, which meant I was to also take care of her. She was a burr under my saddle. She lived in a house on our property—yes, right out my back door—for 25 long, unsettling years until she passed away in a nursing home. Jerry took care of his widowed mother well. He was her son, but I can see that her thumb was on him as much, if not more so, than his was on me.

Now, some of you might be under the impression that the decision to sell that huge 34-foot Class A Winnebago Chieftain motorhome was an easy one for me to make. I mean, it was *Jerry's* dream. Not mine.

But I tossed and turned the idea over in mind until one day, I sat in that monster and cried myself into a doze. When I woke up, I just lay there, staring at the ceiling. I've always looked up at things, so the conglomeration of vents, lights, speakers, and plugs that ran along the roof was not new to me, but the feeling was. All of those things had to be there no matter how undesirable it seemed they were. Like what sometimes I felt my life had been for 40 years.

I thought about all those dreams Jerry had and how I had tried to be excited for them. But I had known, even then, that they were unattainable because, well... money. Then illness and physical capabilities. I could run that motorhome, oh momma, like no one's business. I could drive it, set it up, and prep it for travel. But in the end, it was another one of his dreams, not mine. Like moving to Idaho.

I was beginning to realize that I didn't have to live his dreams anymore. Was it finally time to create some Trina dreams? Could I really do that?

I learned that all of his dreams died with him. All of the things he was had died with him. But I was still trying to live in *his* world, living all the things *he* dreamt of in *his* life. It was a bitter pill to swallow. In that same breath though, I knew then that I could now have some things *I* wanted. Have some of the adventures and treats that were and are just mine.

> **The shift from sad to freeing is slow but real. It takes time, but that's what part of being a widow is like—a little sad and a little freeing.**

I sold that sucker and have moved on to have some amazing Trina road trips. With the cash from the sale of the motorhome, I could stay in nice hotels along the way as I explored my new life. Traveling is fun! I'm nowhere ready to stop!

Of course, that doesn't mean I don't like being at home. I enjoy reconnecting with the friends, especially those since Jerry died (hey, those words are getting easier to say—not all the way, but somewhat easier). I have some wonderful friends who waited for me to come out of my married hidey hole. I have known some of them for more years than there are flavors of ice cream. And they are all just that sweet. But since being widowed, I have discovered something I covet to no end.

I have been adopted.

As a mom.

**As you read about my "kids," know I have changed their names to protect them. Yeah, like they need my protection. YIKERS!

My new family of "my kids" started to develop during the estate sale I held in June the year Jerry died. It was a mad house getting ready, and *Katie*—a very capable young woman—who had worked with us in the hardware store, showed up and just dug right in. She was there until the end, placing stuff to get the best eye appeal and pricing items and making deals left and right. After the sale, she became a part of my life. She was the first peach in my bowl of new kids in my life.

On that same day, *Mark,* a farmer in Diamond Valley who I lovingly call my five-mile neighbor, showed up to load big-ticket items. Mark used both his equipment and mine along his knowledge and powerful strength to load things all day. He still comes over and uses the shop occasionally. It makes me so happy to see, hear, and smell the sounds and smells created from welding and lathe work that drift from the machine shop. My heart sings when I hear work being done in Jerry's shop. Mark knew Jerry, and I like to think he admired his abilities. That pours over onto me. Without being asked, Mark came to help that day in June, resulting in two peaches in my bowl.

Next came *Suzie*, a young lady who lives in town and runs her family's business. I have known of her for many years but mostly from knowing her father. He has since passed away, but I like to think of him as a friend. He and I both had businesses in town and would occasionally run into each other at the post office and talk about life in Eureka. Our local post office is a well-known community place where chitty chat can be seen and heard all day long. Over the years of talking to him, I learned he adored his kids. He was one of those arm's-length friends who I enjoyed talking to over the years.

When he died, his daughter somehow fit into my world. Happenstance would have it that we became friends—where? At the estate sale. Suzie stayed long after the sale to help me put tons of leftover items into the dumpster. I was touched she stuck with me to the end. So much so that she became my third peach.

Luke, who I've known for years, is a little rough around the edges but has become my most enduring of rocks. No matter what's going on in his life, he has dropped everything to come to my aid, cleaned up and ready to receive and give hugs. He has always willingly offered his help and would be so embarrassed to discover I think of him as a peach. But he is, as sweet a peach as has ever been.

I have so many wonderful "kids." How did I fall into this role? How do I deserve so much love and familial warmth?

My "kids" are young with most in their twenties or thirties. Their youth and kindness are good for me and my soul. They have gifted me with renewed life that I still don't think I deserve.

Oh, *Katie, Suzie, Mark*, and *Luke* are just four of my chickadees. I don't have enough fingers to count all who have gathered around me!

And I cherish them. I appreciate their love and concern and try my darndest to reciprocate those feelings. I accept, love, and listen. Listening is the most important thing as I have openly deemed my home a "Free Zone." Free Zone means that no matter what they say to me, I will keep it to myself. I will never pass judgment; I will never share the details of their personal lives or troubles with anyone else. All I want from them is honesty so I can better provide them with a loving ear. Oh, and let me tell you, they have told me things that would set your hair on fire.

They don't want advice, and they don't expect me to make "it" all right. Our Free Zone is where we visit, and I am just an ear. I've found on more than one occasion that really, that's what we all need.

When any of my "kids" start talking things out to me, someone exuding love and understanding, they usually find the answers they need have been there all along the way. Well, I *do* provide a story or two... or twelve from my past that might give them some ideas. I am "the mom," after all!

The first time I received a coffee cup that read "My Mom Is Totally Awesome," I cried like a baby. It's amazing the conversations we've had around my old kitchen table. Again, how did something so wonderful come to find me?

All our married life, I worked with and around men.

Farming, men.

Machine shop, men.

Hardware store, men. Okay, the store was, like, 85 percent male.

When I realized men made up most of my social interactions, I was amazed. After all those years, I'm much more comfortable talking to men than I have ever been talking to women. So, when I woke up alone and discovered I needed friends, I found it difficult to cultivate female relationships.

I've had a few ladies step up—because they needed female friends too!—to become good friends, but it was scary. I always felt as though I had nothing to offer as a woman; truthfully, my self-esteem was nonexistent. But as I ventured farther out of my comfort zone, I found ladies who were just as desperate to make a connection.

Then, there are the men. Happily, I admit I like men. They are fun and funny. Mine was considerate and easy to be around. A bit of a task master, yes, but fun too. And I like to think that I was a good wife and a good woman—a "good catch."

I don't know what will happen in my future. Many widows have adamantly declared they will never pursue another guy for a relationship for the rest of their lives. And that's fine, and I understand that feeling for sure. Me? I'm not going to shut that door. But! I'm also not going to hold it open either. At least not for a while. I've gone on a few outings; I resist calling them dates because I really have no idea what all that should or should not be.

Nevertheless, I learned a couple of important things from these… uh, suitors? Dates? Gentlemen. Let's go with gentlemen.

One of the gentlemen visited me frequently after Jerry's death. While visiting though, he would take time from our scheduled "appointment" to go visit another woman who lived nearby. It took a few repetitions of that behavior before I woke up and told him to hit the road. *Your loss, fella*, I remember thinking.

The other gentleman was a nice guy who I liked and still do. But after all was said and done, I realized I didn't want a long-term thingy. Like I know—well, I think—he did. I don't ever want to be put in the position to take care of another man. I did that, and it was more than I want to ever let happen again. Moreover, I don't ever want to put someone in the position where they have to take care of me when I get old and cranky.

But! I never say never. Too many doors have been shut in my life for me to purposefully close any in front of me. I will just fly by the seat of my pants and happily let life happen. Kinda cool, right? That is the freedom of widowhood.

I would like to have someone to go out with sometimes and maybe do a little traveling with. Only time will tell what the future holds. I am excited to see what waits around every corner of my life. It's just that now, *now* I have the options to pick and choose what corners I want to peek around.

I am in a unique position on the friend front in this way too. I have found wonderful friends through my weekly newspaper column. I am humbled when I gain a good friend through my words. The friends I have been blessed with are true and wonderful people who I feel I can talk to about anything. Both men and women have reached out to me and I am amazed at how kind and giving they can be. Again, how did that happen?

Remember: to have a good friend, you have to first be a good friend.

If you get the chance to surround yourself with people, do it. It really doesn't matter how it happens; let it happen because it's a good thing for your mind, body, and soul. Don't get to the point of not being comfortable saying, "No, thank you," to an invite. Learn to say no and do it with conviction. But be ready to accept invites as well.

I know, I know—it's hard. If you don't say yes, you limit yourself. It's your decision how to spend your widow-y free time. You now have the luxury to say yes or no as you desire. Pretty cool, right?

I have to admit I am happy to be able to come home and be surrounded by my quiet. But! When the quiet gets *too* quiet—and it does more often than I would have imagined—I poke at a friend or two and see what's what in their world. It usually turns into a gab session on the phone or over a grocery run and/or lunch. It takes time to do both.

Get used to the quiet and get used to having freedom to create the noise you need to make you happy. **Your happiness is in your hands and control.**

Grab hold of it and drive it anywhere you want!

19

Tunnel Visionary

At some point, I figured life would begin again. It wasn't daily that I thought this. It was more of a steady push forward. Days, months, then a year came and went. Realization, for me, poked its head in my life's door when I had a problem I could not fix without help. Most everything that spat goo in my face—needing to replace my car; deciding to stay in my home; even changing the oil in my car—all things I could do by myself, gave me strength to "carry on." The things I could conquer by myself gave me hope that I wouldn't be underwater for the rest of my life. Too much time in my silly life was spent chasing that bubble of freedom.

Life for me was never cookie cutter. Oh, there were days of doldrums that seemed to meld together to create the life I had with Jerry. For the most part though, our life had always been one spinning adventure after another. Building a farm life, two very cool but head-banging business ventures, taking vacations, and a lot of little sideline businesses. I know I gave my all to each and every challenge put on my path through life, and I expect that to continue. It is who I am; I love that about my life.

The life and times of Jerry and Trina were lived, for the most part, with no specific agenda. Nothing was ever set in stone. That was the way of life for us even though money was always a *huge* issue. Times were up and down, in and out, over and under. In the end, that is the life that I craved and needed to have. That excitement of life without a roadmap or final plan.

On a cold, quiet January day, I looked back on the three years following his death. Being alone has not changed the fact that I still crave to fly by the seat of my pants! Even so, I still needed a reason, a reason to just be. As the third anniversary of his passing came and went and another winter faded into spring, I found myself without any real plans for the next day, let alone the rest of the year. All I could see were more days of being home and a steady supply of a somewhat sad "just get up and slog through each day" attitude. Yes, true tunnel vision had set in. I saw nothing outside the box of my house. Nothing. That wasn't the person I wanted to become.

Then, in a moment of feeling sorry for myself, I thought about all the things I had done. Okay, all the things I had *accomplished* in those three, short—and long—years. I think I am doing things that, if I were on the outside looking in, I would describe as exciting and boring, hard and easy, sad and happy, right and wrong. I was doing more than just going through the motions.

Then another "ta-da" moment hit me. In short, I began the act of living. Wow, how did that happen? I was living again.

I have told people that I have known other women who have lost their husbands and a few men who have lost their wives. It seemed to me that some of them would just become stuck. Not going forward to live again. Yes, nearly all of them have kids and then grandkids, and that easily became their life. If that was their life before becoming a widow and that was the life they loved, I give kudos for living exactly what they envisioned. However, I don't have kids, and I like to think that even if I did, I wouldn't get stuck in the life *we* were going to have. No, I want the life *I* want. The problem as I saw it was that I had absolutely no idea what that life, the life of Trina, was supposed to be.

I set out to find me.

Oh, that sounds so self-serving. I know I am way more comfortable being the giver than the taker in life. So that change, looking at my wants and needs instead of everyone else's, took some getting used to.

A farmer friend shared this story with me one day a few years into my widowhood. A short time after Jerry passed, a group of men from the valley where we lived converged on a corner to discuss farming and the events of the world and of our Diamond Valley. Apparently, my name came up.

131

At that, I laughed. "Just mine? Not Jerry's?"

Our mutual friend laughed because it was never just me; it was usually just Jerry—and sometimes Trina. He went on to explain that one of the men wondered what would happen to me, what I would do. My future came up and something about maybe someday there would be a new *whoever* in my life. Then one of the farmers said, "Oh, don't worry. Trina will always be Jerry's girl."

I was flattered—and taken aback. Would I never just be Trina? That made me realize that I had to work toward becoming me, just me. Just *me* for *me*. I have to say that to myself, "just for me," over and over again.

To think of me and my wants and needs? I was afraid to be seen as selfish. But to move forward, I had to do things just for me and not worry how it looked to others. Then I realized I am not the center of the universe. That I could be self-serving and none of the seven billion other people in the rest of the world would care. Oh yes, I would care, but the world would not give a hoot.

In my zeal to not get stuck, I may have moved faster than the "norm" after becoming a widow. That's when I found there truly was no norm. There was an unwritten rule to "not do anything for at least a year." But a year can be a life sentence. In a year, a ton of stuff happens, and the days that go by are not days you can ever get back. Like, if you sit and watch the second hand on a clock. Quickly, the clock ticks away 47 seconds. Suddenly, all of those seconds are gone, forever. I thought about the "norm" and then jumped into life as it spat at me over and over again.

Jerry died in January; by April of that year, I found myself at a photography seminar because a friend I met through my column and who lives in Southern California had cajoled me into going. I don't think she knew exactly how new into widowhood I was. That shell-shattering seminar was held in Winnemucca, Nevada about 200 miles away. On the morning I left, I was so scared. The trip took me north on a small state highway to where I would get onto Interstate 80, a freeway. It was a route I knew well.

Just as I turned onto the on-ramp, my phone rang, so I pulled over. It was a cousin of Jerry's who I have now adopted as my own. I answered, and when I heard her voice, I started to cry. Like I've said many times, I am such a girl. I blubbered to her asking why I was going to this thingy. What in the world was I thinking? I just wanted to turn around and go home and crawl into my shell and never come out.

She talked me down off the proverbial ledge. I can see now that He was definitely in on the conversation as I sobbed in my truck along the freeway crowded with cars and trucks of people all heading somewhere to do something. All those people were moving along with life.

As she and I talked, I knew that if I turned around, I would never move forward. Oh, it would have been so easy to go home. Just put blinders on and keep my head down and not look around at what the world had to offer. Keep my head in the tunnel and have nothing but safe comfortable tunnel vision. We talked for about 30 minutes before I was composed enough to carry on with not only that trip and weekend, but my life.

I was as nervous as a baby bird perched on the edge of the nest, ready to take to the air. Wings all a twitter, stretching out for that first flight. Beak pointed into the wind ready to catch a breeze to steady those new wings. April sun shining on my face, I drove on and with the push of my wonderful cousin, I flew into my newness.

You should never—I repeat, *never*—let an opportunity pass you by. Uh, unless it's illegal. HEE. HEE. HEE. If I would have turned around on that wonderful spring day, I would have missed out on learning about photography and myself. I still know next to nothing about taking pictures, but I like to think I know a bit more about myself. And I made some new friends that weekend! I stepped out of my shell and left tunnel vision in my rearview mirror of life.

It was nerve wracking and heart pounding, but hey, getting that heart of yours to pound cleans out all the pipes. It covers you with something I apparently needed, self-confidence. And you have it too. It's in there somewhere. You just have to open the door to let it in and push yourself out into the world.

When you are ready—oh, you'll be ready—get out there!

Tunnel vision is the lack of seeing anything in your peripheral. Seeing just what is in front and not taking in everything that is around you. If you can only see straight forward, it stands to reason that you might only see what is directly behind you too. I found often that when I looked forward, it seemed that looking back was also the only thing in my line of sight. It really was like tunnel vision.

Observing what was in my life turned into what would *only* be in my future. I knew only a straight line, what I had done up until that point. And that was being stuck. Then I went to that seminar and magically, the tunnel gave way to a field.

I had to remember my own advice: "Don't look back, Trina. You're not going that way!" Holding my head up and looking around was amazing. There was a huge, wonderfully open world out there, at my feet. Just waiting for me.

Yes, over that weekend I learned a little about picture taking. Even learned a few things about my little red camera and I have taken some pretty cool pictures since that eye-opening experience.

I now know I am *not* a photographer. I am a picture taker. I take pictures because I want to see that sight again and again. It is not my calling though. More than learning about picture taking, I learned I could move on and be anything I wanted as long as I was willing to work toward my desire.

I love to cook, mostly comfort food. I love to garden—uh, flowers not vegetables. I love to take walks, only when it is warm. I love to drive, to get somewhere fun. I sort of like to talk. No, let me be perfectly clear on this one: I *love* to talk. Knowing all that about me and having an outlet to talk with words has afforded me an opportunity to move forward with my life. I could have just as easily found my calling in owning a restaurant. Or I could have, as the Aussies say, taken a walk about for as long and as far as my little footsies would have carried me. But it was words that made me happy. And words allow me to reach out and touch as many lives as are willing to be a part of my world.

To that end, after friends' pushing and prodding, I decided to try my hand at a book. I am a great believer in the old adage "Write what you know." So, I joyfully put together a collection of my columns that made me smile. It was such a learning experience to see just how far I could push myself to learn about the business end of writing. Soon, my first book *They Call Me Weener: 55 Giggle Producing Chinwags* was born and out on Amazon.com.

But as exciting as it was to push the "publish" button, I cried too. I cried for me. Because I sat in my house, alone, at my table with my laptop in front of me, pushing a button that put my first book out into the world—and there was nobody around to celebrate with me. So, yes, I cried happy, sad, mad, soul-crushing tears.

Then, just as you will when faced with such heart-ripping things and times, I pulled myself up and looked at the fact that I accomplished something amazing. You will too. Whatever it is that you take a stab at and that stabs you back. **Take a look at what you have done. By yourself.** Oh, we so got this new life.

Over the years in my spare time, I would read all I could about writing and the ins and outs of being a writer. It's a quiet, solitary existence with spots of exuberance throughout the process. Then, there was the idea of learning more about the craft and finding opportunities to get to know other writers. That was my next step, actually going to a writer's workshop. Hey, what a way to get myself out of my solitude and see what's what in an activity of my choice!

If I had chosen quilting, I would have looked for a quilting bee. If I had chosen to pursue studies in nuclear physics… well, I have no idea what I would have done. So, it's a good thing I didn't go *that* way. No, writing is what I like and what I wanted to do with most of my time. Probably not the best choice for my physical self, all that sitting while writing. Not really all that butt friendly, you know! But the outcome, I think, is worth the choice.

Creating something from nothing that has the possibility of making someone smile or is in some tiny way helpful? That's pretty heady stuff to me. I strive for that with each word, sentence, and story. With writing, I can stop anytime I want and take that walk in the sunshine. Or garden my flowers, or cook, or talk. For me, writing called me back into life.

It's so easy to say, "Not today," or "No thanks" to an invitation. To see an upcoming event that looks so inviting is as terrifying to me as it is exciting. As embarrassing as it is to admit, I have even let invitations slide and apologized afterwards. It's gotten easier as time marches along to agree to engagements that, just a short time ago, I would have run and hid from. I was keeping my tunnel vision 20-20. That had to change.

The worst thing I found about not accepting an invitation or missing an opportunity to go somewhere and do something is not the guilt; it's the sadness of missing the opportunity. I have to remind myself that that sadness will come if I don't do something that pushes me outside my comfort zone. So, again: **when you're ready, get out there!**

You'll be interested—or maybe not—to learn that my fear pushed me into agreeing to, at the tender age of 65, go skydiving. Oh, you bet your sweet Bippy I went. Other than racing a car out on a highway at 2 a.m. as a teenager or driving the car endowed with the name The Bippy Mobile, which a friend and I built and I drove in a demolition derby when I was 19, skydiving was one of the most amazing things I've ever done. And if I were asked to race a car, drive in a derby, or jump out of a perfectly good airplane again? Are you kidding me! I would happily do them all again. Again and again.

It was also that push which took me to my first writer's conference in Las Vegas the month after I went to the photography seminar. I decided there would be no moss growing under my newly-widowed feet. But talk about being out of my element. Holy cats!

It's not that we all don't belong in meetings or conferences or parties or any other assemblies of people with whom we share interests. It's the fear of the act of getting us into the situations that is the culprit. The act of not acting on our desires, that's the thief stealing our experiences we crave. Not only as new widows or widowers, but as people.

Life found me being the quintessential wallflower. Playing it safe with my back against the wall. Not stepping out just to be tripped up by some self-issued, disparaging image of myself and falling flat on my face in front of everyone.

Now?

Now, I take great pleasure in putting my face out into the crowd. It has taken me blankity-blank years, but my face is now turned outward toward the crowd instead of pressed against a wall. One of the many, many things I have learned since becoming a onesome is this: nobody is there to push me forward. I have to push myself out into life. That is very, very hard. For everyone. In that same respect, there is no one there to stop you from moving forward—no one but yourself. I just had to get out of my own way to move forward.

That first writer's conference I went to was hard. It was not an easy thing to see myself stepping into a big room full of people who have made their way in the craft I had chosen to be part of. I had no idea how to act, how to be a real writer. Writing, publishing, marketing, and—oh, my stars—a platform with

Facebook and Twitter and all things which any 12-year-old would know everything about. I had, and still have, no idea about those things. My first step was to figure out just how to go about signing up for the Las Vegas Writers Conference. I was not born into the computer world, and I do not have the aforementioned 12-year-old to call for help to come do computer things for me. Push. Push. Push forward.

I was so full of myself when I found the website. From there, it took me about a week, maybe more, to figure it all out. Where, when, what to sign up for. Sure, now looking back I made way too much out of that process. It was a maze to me then. Without anyone to push me, I had to push myself. It came down to talking to myself.

"Sit down, Trina. Look. Concentrate."

Then to finally figure out what I wanted to see and do and learn, then put stuff in my cart and do that final "click here to buy" was one giant step for this chick-a-dee. I'm here to tell you I sweated bullets just getting signed up. Then to go! My knees shook, and my heart hammered; my guilt was immense.

This was all about me.

All just for Trina.

None of it had anything to do with Jerry. That had *never* happened in all of my married life. Anything that was scheduled was, in reality, always surrounded by something *he* wanted to do or somewhere *he* wanted or *we* needed to go. This was all Trina from beginning to end. All of it was so, so—well, honestly—it was all so cool. I pushed myself forward at every opportunity. I still do. Does that make me a pushy broad?

AARRGGHH What a scary thing it all was. But I did it. I went. I mingled. I learned some stuff. Then I came home and cried yet again. This time though, I cried at the new happy I had created and felt inside of me. It was guilt, but it was happy too. I was moving forward.

Looking back, when it came time to load up and go to Las Vegas, being the girl I am, I sat in the car before leaving the yard and cried. Geeze Louise, that seems to be a theme with me. I say it's because I am a girl, and I wholeheartedly believe it is that. But also, it's because of guilt. Of not making the best of my life up until that exact moment.

Even now, I feel like I don't have the right to have this much fun with my life—because all it took was for my husband to die. That's a lot to carry around. Talk about baggage!

It is what it is.

That's a truism. Guilt at being happy may lessen over time, but it will probably always be there. For me, and you too I would bet. To have the life we now have, something huge had to happen.

Remember this though. **They died; _we_ did not.** We are still sucking air every single day.

When we open our eyes in the morning, we still see the green of the grass, not the brown under it. We still see the sunrise and the moon come up. We still have the bills and the trials and tribulations of life. Knowing that, know this too—**it is more than okay to have some happy in life.**

Only you will know when you are ready, then…

Get Out There and Lay Claim to Your Happy.

20

The Turn at the End of the Road

Remember when you really wanted something as a kid and you would whine to your mom, "But Mooomm! Everybody else gets to stay out after nine!" I would hasten to say her pat response was exactly what her mom had probably told her: "If everybody jumped off a bridge, would you jump off a bridge too?" That is on my mind every time I want to generalize or group people together. But! Here is one that I feel is true to its core, and everybody can say it.

My experience of life is mine, and *nobody* will ever know what it's like, feel how it feels, see, want, or get to be me.

It isn't about fixing what is wrong. This widow stuff isn't something anyone can "fix." Really, it isn't even about trying to make it easier to go through or live with. It's more, in my very humble opinion, like getting along with it all. The shock, heartache, surprise, anger, loneliness, relief, and—in the end—"re-life" which will come and go and go and come back. It's all a push that can be felt once in a while, or once a day, or at first constantly. It's a slap in the face when you see a picture, hear a laugh, smell a smell.

When I was young and lost my first baby to a miscarriage, I fell apart. Then it happened again and again and yet a fourth time. All within a year, yes one year. I remember someone, who had a passel of children, telling me they couldn't understand how I could keep going after loving and losing something that had once been a part of me. It took a while, but I finally realized that I have loved and lost—and that sad never really gets better. It does, however, thankfully get farther away. Of course, you can still see them, feel them. But they're not as immediate, as painful.

I will always have the opportunity to say things like, "In two days, it will…" I was going to say it will be our 45th wedding anniversary. But it won't, will it? It's no longer *our* anything.

Such days will come for you—yes, they will come, and they will go.

Remember, the sun will pop up again and shine on your face.

I recently passed that realization along to one of my newly "adopted" daughters, Katie. I was pleased I could use my current circumstances to help her. Oh, that makes me smile from here to the moon. Maybe that's one of the reasons I am here, in my new widow shoes.

Katie, my little chick-a-dee of a daughter, lost her very best friend to that awful scourge, breast cancer. Those two girls, young women really, were quite a pair and close as two peas in a very happy pod. Then her lovely friend, who it just so happens was also another daughter from another mother of mine, died. The one left behind to live life without her "sister," my sweet young girl, had such a hard time dealing with not only losing her bestie but her best friend's widowed husband, who fell away from her as a result.

He moved on with his life and fell in love with another woman. The fact that he could just move on tore my sad chick-a-dee daughter up inside. But beyond the sadness, she was furious. All she could perceive was him spitting on the loving image of her friend. And the woman in question, the new love, was a poisonous vixen moving in on her friend's territory.

All of those things tore at her. Her anger was so real and so huge that she just couldn't stand by and watch. Midnight anger is awful. Midnight anger will ask you to do things you would not

141

ordinarily do. In her anger, she began losing herself in this man's life and his decisions. She wanted to do something, *anything*, to stop this new widower from moving away from what he and her friend had—in the past. I am so thankful she reached out to me.

In helping her, I helped myself see that it was the way of life to move on. To go forward. To not become stuck in the muck of sadness and memories. I could hear myself talking to my own heart. In the back and forth with her, I suddenly saw that I was finally okay with my new life. What did I tell her? What nuggets of gold did I bestow on her?

I told her that I loved her and loved that she held onto the memories of the life she had lost with her dearest friend. All of what her friend was, who she was, all the things she did and of all the things they had done together. That all the things that friend owned and wanted, all of that was now gone. Oh, you will never forget the life that is no more, but that life ended and will never again be a part of her, or me, or the man who was her husband. A very sad but real realization for her and for me.

In regards to me and Jerry... Will I ever forget all the times I made margaritas and tacos for us? Will I ever forget the time I threw a cup of ice at him because he went on and on about spending money for a camp trailer that we could not afford? Will I ever forget his easy smile and hidden laugh that I only really saw him let go of once in all those years? No. No. No.

On the other hand, will I now have to get up every morning, every single morning, to have Jerry be the first thing I think of? Will all the things he bought and collected and that I see every day always be his?

And this big one.

Will I always be Jerry's girl?

Again, the answers to these questions are, No. No. No.

It is not my responsibility but my *choice* to stand on my own two feet and live as a one instead of half of a two that is no longer there.

I wish I had told her this story as it tells of growing away from that "once was" life and moving on to stand on one's own two feet.

Among the hundreds of old western shows Jerry liked to watch was *The Rifleman*. Might have something to do with the Winchester rifle that Lucas McCain carried as Jerry loved old Winchesters. The plot followed the adventures of a widower and his son and all they endured after the woman, the wife and mother, died. The thing that stood out to me when I watched "his" show for the first time after Jerry's death, was the kid's determination to keep alive some flowers. I thought, *Oh, how sweet.*

The first year after Jerry died, I let his garden go and grow anything that was going to come up on its own. It's called letting things come up volunteer. No planting or planning. Things just went to seed and those seeds voluntarily came up hither and yon.

He had built raised beds for me—well, us—but I had laid claim to a smaller one for flowers. His was bigger, longer, and just the right height for him to work on while riding on his scooter. He was a farmer; it was in his blood, and he farmed that bed every day like it was a thousand acres. Getting the soil ready. Planting seeds, and yes, some wonderful gladiolus that he entered into the fair in huge colorful displays. The rest of the bed was planted to vegetables.

He always grew more than the two of us could ever eat. It wasn't for the food that he grew things. It was the act of getting out and being alive that he kept his garden going. In some ways, that raised bed of his kept him going for years too. Then, that last summer was more than he could keep up with. The lettuce went to seed. He didn't dig up his gladiolus bulbs to save for the next season, and he didn't harvest the last of his kale. I have to tell you, I do not like kale. So, the next year the lettuce just came up, everywhere. The gladiolus bulbs froze and died. The kale he loved came back too. A lot of kale!

I don't like kale. I didn't ever like the lettuce from the garden because it was always full of earwigs. Just saying. Anyway.

I watered it all and just let it all come up voluntary that first summer, and it was actually very pretty. Along with the kale and the lettuce that bloomed these tiny little cotton-like puffs of flowers, a few radishes grew freely. In the menagerie, a couple of carrots and masses of cilantro showed me their fern-like greenery. And one silly potato plant. I do think that one potato was from Jerry as he was from Idaho, and I occasionally called him my Idaho spud!

Midsummer, a lady friend was thinning out her white iris bed so she brought me a few buckets full of plants. I dug out some mushy gladiolus bulbs he had on one end of the vegetable planter and planted her gift to me in their place. I smiled as I watched them take root and grow. Toward the end of the year, I started to pull up the lettuce plants, and I took some seeds from the flowers from the perennial plants in my "flowers only" bed and threw them in the bed that was his vegetables only and began to make it mine. Just mine. Like everything else we had—it was now, just mine.

The second spring, I was blessed by the seeds I had tossed over to that veggie bed as they began growing and grew wonderful plants that began blooming. Then those white irises grew and delivered some wonderful blossoms during the summer. But his kale also came back. That made me happy in its strength. During that year, I did something I hadn't done in years—I bought some bedding plants, just flowers though. Summertime, I grew wonderful flowers which drew in butterflies and bees and humming birds galore. None of which seemed to like the kale either, and that made me laugh. Yes, I laughed out loud. Of course, I cried too.

At the end of that second year, I dug out the icky kale and planted a new Shasta daisy in its place. I know that daisy will come back year after year. It will draw butterflies and bees and hummingbirds to its sweet flowers. Jerry always wore a red baseball type cap. It was like his signature. You could pick him out of any crowd by his cap. He had one that was clean, for going to town, and one that was dirty for work. The dirty one had unmistakable marks on the brim where his working-man dirty and greasy fingers always grabbed it as he took it off and put it on. No matter which one he wore, out in the yard every summer, the

144

hummingbirds would divebomb and buzz him, thinking he was the hummingbird feeder. Sometimes they would even get right up to the brim of his hat and look him right in the eye. Now that daisy would bring humming birds in close and make me smile with that memory.

How could I ever forget all he was? I will not forget him completely; he will just get farther away. I will always talk about him. Just not as frequently as time goes on. I will always want him back. I will not, however, close the door to the wonderful things that will happen in my life from now until my life ends.

I took a different road with the raised-bed garden. Now, I use the space to grow flowers that make me happy. All of the roads in front of me will certainly have some ruts and potholes. I will certainly stumble and fall. I will certainly have happy in my life. I will travel them all and make the most of each turn and curve and stop sign. I will not miss another stop sign. They apparently are put in front of me to make me slow down and look both ways. Just for me.

Yes, now it is really all about just me. Not us, just me.

That's what I told her to usher her forward in life without her friend. I pray it helped her see that the man who was married to her dear friend was also moving forward with his life, without Katie's lost friend. Like she now needed to do.

Hang on!
We are almost done. Almost to the end of this journey together and the beginning of your new life.

I hope and pray.

When I sit down to pray, I visualize three doors in front of me. Doors of my past, present, and future. First, I thank Him for my past, and I try to think of one tiny memory from over the years. He never disappoints me with a memory. Then I thank Him for my present, and I think of something going on in my life. Then. This one makes me all giddy. I thank Him for my future.

In my head when I think of what is to come, I see that future door in front of me. That door is the only one I seem to want to open. I know behind that door lays wonderment. Good and bad, I'm sure. I reach my hand out to touch it, to open that door. The door to my future is made of brown-streaked, weathered wood and has a ruddy black, wrought-iron door knob. I am so close, I can feel the warmth from the wood and the coolness of the iron.

I am reaching as far as my arm will stretch. I want to see what is behind that big door. Yet, I'm terrified to know what awaits me. It's so close but so far away. Yes, like that bubble.

Then, as I breathe, the door floats away and I say, "Thank you, God, for my life, my past, my present, and my future. Amen."

Be Happy, Happy All the Time

T.

About The Author

Trina came into the world in Reno, Nevada in 1955, exactly six months between Christmases on June 25. It was snowing as her mother was playing the slot machines in the newly-opened John Ascuaga's Nugget that June! In the late sixties, her family moved to the tiny town of Ely, Nevada where she went to high school, graduating from White Pine High School in 1973. Go Bobcats!

Trina's writing career began in her formative years but was put on the back-burner for the next work-filled, 40-plus years until she bulldozed herself into her local newspaper in 2012 with her dream column "Is This You?" She self-syndicated "Is This You?" which can now be found in several newspapers and is growing as fast as she can stick her foot into newspaper editors' doors.

Since that first column, a tiny voice has screamed at her to write, to complete the ultimate author dream of publishing a book. That happened in 2020 with her first book *They Call Me Weener: 55 Giggle Producing Chinwags*. Well, of course her book can be found online wherever books are sold. Or as she likes to tout, email her at itybytrina@yahoo.com for a signed copy. Now, this second book *Life After a Death* has her reaching for the stars as she hopes it will help others. She is already zipping words out for her third book.

After becoming a widow in 2018, she grabbed hold of life and decided that being stuck in the sad was not something she wanted. The up-down merry-go-round isn't just about being a widow; it's about being part of a new amazing life.

Trina now lives in Diamond Valley just north of Eureka, Nevada where she has been for over 45 years. Trina has focused on living—writing more, doing the things she only dreamt of doing during those wedded years, and honoring her life as Jerry's wife. Trina doesn't have many regrets except letting all those years go by without being able to write about them. That is where she gets most of the fuel for her "Is This You?" column. The future holds only new experiences to write and giggle about with her friends and readers.

Trina went skydiving for her 65th birthday! Always looking forward to the next adventure, she is constantly encouraged by her circle of grand friends that pull and push her when her feet stumble. She often sings of how blessed she is to have been gifted with the talent of writing but very rarely knows how a story will end. (She says she sings only when by herself because even the neighboring cats howl at the caterwauling.)

Trina humbly chalks up her writing talent up to her faith; her talent is God's way of telling her she is alive. Truly, Trina is one person who is—yep…

Happy, Happy All the Time.

"The Blue Box"

It's Christmas time. A time of good cheer, merriment and warm fuzzy feelings. I do not forget the reason for the season. The birth of my Savior. But I also am inclined to enjoy the warmth of all that the season offers. Friends, family, food, frivolity and—decorating. More so in years past, but still I trudge out to the storage shed and retrieve the priceless family decorations. Now why is this of such importance to write about? What is it that makes this annual event noteworthy? It's the blue box...

To download a free copy of Trina's Christmas story mentioned on page 116, visit:

https://dl.bookfunnel.com/pqxw9erzj1

www.ingramcontent.com/pod-product-compliance
Lightning Source LLC
Chambersburg PA
CBHW070934030426
42336CB00014BA/2675